Peter Grieder offers a thought-provoking introduction to the history of East Germany which engages critically with key debates and advances fresh interpretations. Arguing that the German Democratic Republic (GDR) was a totalitarian welfare state, Grieder:

- divides its life into six phases: conception, construction, consolidation, conservatism, crisis, and collapse
- analyses key concepts in the Introduction
- provides an overall assessment of the GDR at the end of the volume
- integrates GDR popular opinion in order to gain a deeper understanding of the East German polity.

Clear, concise, and up to date, this is an essential new study for anyone with an interest in the origins, development, and ultimate downfall of the self-proclaimed 'Workers' and Peasants' Power'.

Peter Grieder is Lecturer in Twentieth-Century History at the University of Hull. His previous publications include *The East German Leadership, 1946–1973: Conflict and Crisis* (1999).

Studies in European History are designed to present the 'state of the debate' on important themes and episodes in European history since the sixteenth century in a clear and critical way for students. Each book carries its own interpretations and conclusions, while locating the discussion firmly in the centre of the current issues as historians see them.

Studies in European History

Studies in European History
Series Standing Order ISBN 0–333–79365–X
(outside North America only)

You can receive future titles in this series as they are published by placing a standing order. Please contact your bookseller or, in case of difficulty, write to us at the address below with your name and address, the title of the series and the ISBN quoted above.

Customer Services Department, Macmillan Distribution Ltd
Houndmills, Basingstoke, Hampshire RG21 6XS, England

The German Democratic Republic

Peter Grieder

palgrave
macmillan

First published 2012 by
PALGRAVE MACMILLAN

Palgrave Macmillan in the UK is an imprint of Macmillan Publishers Limited, registered in England, company number 785998, of Houndmills, Basingstoke, Hampshire RG21 6XS.

Palgrave Macmillan in the US is a division of St Martin's Press LLC, 175 Fifth Avenue, New York, NY 10010.

Palgrave Macmillan is the global academic imprint of the above companies and has companies and representatives throughout the world.

Palgrave® and Macmillan® are registered trademarks in the United States, the United Kingdom, Europe and other countries.

ISBN 978–0–230–57937–8

This book is printed on paper suitable for recycling and made from fully managed and sustained forest sources. Logging, pulping and manufacturing processes are expected to conform to the environmental regulations of the country of origin.

A catalogue record for this book is available from the British Library.

A catalog record for this book is available from the Library of Congress.

10 9 8 7 6 5 4 3 2 1
21 20 19 18 17 16 15 14 13 12
Printed in China

To my beloved brother, Robert, who died suddenly on the night of 15–16 February 2011

Contents

Contents

Contents

Note on References

References are cited throughout in square brackets according to the numbering in the bibliography.

Editors' Preface

The Studies in European History series offers a guide to develop-ments in a field of history that has become increasingly specialized with the sheer volume of new research and literature now pro-duced. Each book has three main objectives. The primary purpose is to offer an informed assessment of opinion on a key episode or theme in European history. Secondly, each title presents a dis-tinct interpretation and conclusions from someone who is closely involved with current debates in the field. Thirdly, it provides stu-dents and teachers with a succinct introduction to the topic, with the essential information necessary to understand it and the litera-ture being discussed. Equipped with an annotated bibliography and other aids to study, each book provides an ideal starting point from which to explore important events and processes that have shaped Europe's history to the present day.

Books in the series introduce students to historical approaches which in some cases are very new and which, in the normal course of things, would take many years to filter down to textbooks. By presenting history's cutting edge, we hope that the series will dem-onstrate some of the excitement that historians, like scientists, feel as they work on the frontiers of their subjects. The series also has an important contribution to make in publicizing what historians are doing, and making it accessible to students and scholars in this and related disciplines.

John Breuilly
Julian Jackson
Peter H. Wilson

Acknowledgements

First and foremost, I thank Professor Peter H. Wilson, GF Grant Professor of History at the University of Hull, for proposing that I write this book. His advice, both as a colleague and as one of the Series Editors, has been invaluable. I also thank the two other Series Editors, John Breuilly and Julian Jackson, for their very helpful suggestions. MPS Limited assisted me in compiling the index and for this I am most grateful. A particular debt of gratitude is owed to Sonya Barker, the Senior Editor of Humanities at Palgrave Macmillan, for all her patience and support over the past four years.

In Chapters 5 and 6 I draw somewhat on my piece in McDermott, Kevin and Matthew Stibbe (eds.), *Revolution and Resistance in Eastern Europe: Challenges to Communist Rule* (Oxford and NY, 2006). See Peter Grieder, '"To Learn from the Soviet Union is to Learn How to Win": The East German Revolution, 1989–90', pp. 157–74. I thank the editors and Berg Publishers for granting me permission to reuse the material. I am also grateful to Manchester University Press for allowing me to repeat words and arguments from my 1999 monograph, *The East German Leadership, 1946–1973: Conflict and Crisis*. Furthermore, I express my appreciation to the journal *Central European History* and its publisher Cambridge University Press for permitting me to reuse sentences from my 2005 review of Hope M. Harrison's seminal work, *Driving the Soviets up the Wall: Soviet-East German Relations, 1953–1961*.

Last but not least, I would like to thank the University of Hull for helping to make this book possible.

Abbreviations and Glossary

Abgrenzung	The SED's policy of disassociating the GDR from any notion of a shared German culture with the FRG, pursued with particular vigour after 1971.
Bezirk (plural *Bezirke*)	Regional administrative district of the GDR, 1952–90. There were 14 until East Berlin, officially referred to as 'Berlin', was added in 1961.
Bonn Republic	Same as the FRG.
bourgeois parties	Non-Communist parties allied to the SED as part of the 'Democratic Bloc'. Also known as Bloc Parties. They included the CDU and the LDPD.
CDU	*Christlich-Demokratische Union* (Christian Democratic Union).
Central Committee	National leadership body of Communist Parties such as the SED.
Combat Groups of the Working Class	*Kampfgruppen der Arbeiterklasse* (SED-controlled militias organized at factories and other workplaces across East Germany).
Comecon	Council for Mutual Economic Assistance: a Soviet-led trading bloc of Communist countries established in 1949 and dissolved in 1991.

Cominform	Communist Bureau of Information, 1947–56.
Council of Ministers	The East German government. Its Chairman was Prime Minister of the GDR.
Council of State or State Council	The institution that replaced the GDR Presidency in 1960. Its Chairman was effectively Head of State.
CPSU	Communist Party of the Soviet Union.
CSSR	Czechoslovak Socialist Republic (1960–90).
détente	Thaw in Superpower relations during the 1970s.
Deutsche Außenpolitik	'German Foreign Policy': a GDR newspaper.
Eastern bloc	The states of Eastern and Central Europe which were part of the Soviet empire from the late 1940s until its collapse in 1989–91.
East Germany	Same as the GDR.
ESS	Economic System of Socialism (the SED's economic reform programme, 1967–71).
FDGB	*Freier Deutscher Gewerkschaftsbund* (League of Free German Trade Unions).
FDJ	*Freie Deutsche Jugend* (Free German Youth).
FRG	Federal Republic of Germany, also known as West Germany or the Bonn Republic. Often referred to simply as the Federal Republic.
Frieden schaffen ohne Waffen	Create Peace Without Weapons (East Germany's unofficial peace movement founded by the Protestant Church in 1980).
GDR	German Democratic Republic, also known as East Germany.
glasnost	Soviet leader Mikhail Gorbachev's policy of openness introduced in the USSR after 1985.
HVA	*Hauptverwaltung Aufklärung* (Main Administration for Reconnaissance: the Stasi's foreign intelligence service).
IM	*Inoffizieller Mitarbeiter* ('unofficial collaborator' of the Stasi).

KGB	Committee for State Security of the USSR.
KPD	*Kommunistische Partei Deutschlands* (Communist Party of Germany).
Land (plural *Länder*)	State, province, or region of the Soviet Occupation Zone / GDR, 1945–52. All five were restored just before German reunification in 1990.
LDPD	*Liberal-Demokratische Partei Deutschlands* (Liberal Democratic Party of Germany).
mass organizations	Official organizations for the masses allied to the SED. These included the Free German Youth (FDJ) and Free German Trade Union Federation (FDGB).
MfS	*Ministerium für Staatssicherheit* (the GDR's Ministry for State Security, also known as the Stasi or 'Firm').
MVD	Ministry of Internal Affairs (Soviet Union).
National Defence Council	Established in 1960 as the highest state institution of the GDR responsible for national defence. Its Chairman was effectively East Germany's Commander-in-Chief.
National Front	A united front of anti-fascist parties and mass organizations under the auspices of the SED. It had committees at district, local and neighbourhood level. During national and local government elections, it presented a single list of candidates and a single electoral programme.
NATO	North Atlantic Treaty Organization set up in 1949.
NES	New Economic System (the SED's economic reform programme, 1963–7).
Neues Deutschland	'New Germany': the SED's daily newspaper.
Notgemeinschaft	Community born of necessity.
NKVD	Soviet People's Commissariat for Internal Affairs, the Soviet secret police (until 1954) and predecessor of the KGB.

NSDAP

Nationalsozialistische Deutsche Arbeiterpartei (National Socialist German Workers' Party, more commonly known as the Nazi Party).

NVA

Nationale Volksarmee (the GDR's National People's Army).

OECD

Organization for Economic Cooperation and Development.

'Ostalgie'

'Nostalgia for the East': nostalgia for certain aspects of the defunct SED regime.

Ostpolitik

'Eastern policy' introduced during the late 1960s: West Germany's policy of rapprochement towards the Soviet bloc in general and the GDR in particular.

Party Conference

An official gathering of SED delegates sometimes called between Party Congresses.

Party Congress

An official meeting of Communist Party delegates held every four or five years.

Party of the new type

Party based on the CPSU model.

People's Democracy

The Communist description of the system of government in Eastern Europe from the late 1940s until 1989, according to which 'democratic power' was vested in 'the people' rather than 'the bourgeoisie'.

People's Police

Volkspolizei (the national police force of the GDR, organized on a semi-military basis).

perestroika

Soviet leader Mikhail Gorbachev's policy of restructuring introduced in the USSR after 1985.

Politburo

The supreme policy-making committee of Communist Parties such as the SED.

Rechtsstaat

A state under the rule of law.

Schicksalsgemeinschaft

Community of fate.

SED

Sozialistische Einheitspartei Deutschlands (Socialist Unity Party of Germany, the ruling party of the GDR. Its General Secretary, known as First Secretary between 1953 and 1976, was the most powerful person in East Germany).

SMAD	*Sowjetische Militäradministration in Deutschland* (Soviet Military Administration in Germany).
'*Sonderweg*'	Special path (Germany's 'peculiar', illiberal road to modernity compared to Western countries such as Britain and France).
Soviet bloc	Same as the Eastern bloc.
SPD	*Sozialdemokratische Partei Deutschlands* (Social Democratic Party of Germany).
Der Spiegel	'The Mirror': a West German weekly magazine.
Stasi	Acronym for *Staatssicherheit(sdienst)* or 'State Security (Service)': commonly used name for the MfS.
State Planning Commission	A GDR government body responsible for setting economic targets.
Unrechtsstaat	A state of injustice.
USA	United States of America.
USSR	Union of Soviet Socialist Republics (the Soviet Union).
Volkskammer	People's Chamber: East Germany's parliament.
Wende	'Change' or 'turn': often used to denote the 1989–90 Revolution in the GDR.
Warsaw Pact	Military alliance of the Soviet bloc, 1955–91.
West Germany	Same as the FRG and the Bonn Republic.
Workers' and Peasants' Power	The GDR as depicted by its leaders.
Workers' and Peasants' State	Same as the Workers' and Peasants' Power.
'*Zwangsvereinigung*'	Forced union of the SPD and KPD in the Soviet Occupation Zone, 1946.

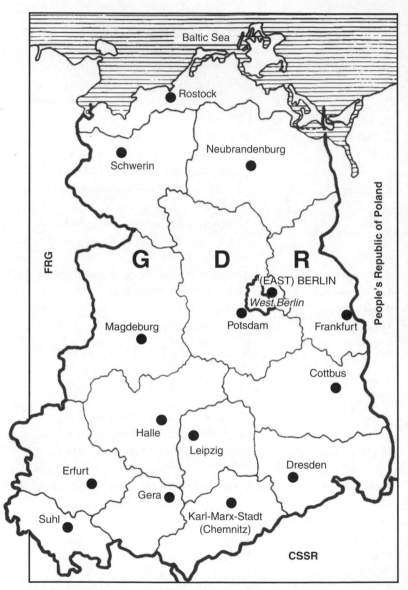

The German Democratic Republic, its *Bezirke*, and their capital cities, 1952–1990 (adapted from map in [8: 175]).

Introduction: Concepts

Dictatorship

Despite its middle name, the German Democratic Republic (GDR) was a Communist dictatorship from the day it was founded on 7 October 1949. This is hardly disputed by historians. When East Germans went to the polls, they could not change their government or even alter the balance of forces within it. The Marxist–Leninist 'Socialist Unity Party of Germany' (SED) always occupied a hegemonic position within the political system and its 'leading role' was enshrined in the 1968 and 1974 constitutions. As for the so-called bourgeois parties and mass organizations, they were satellites of the Communists. Before 13 August 1961 the only way of voting meaningfully was with one's feet, but even that possibility was removed once the Berlin Wall went up. Power was concentrated in the SED Politburo, often referred to as the 'Council of Gods' [39: 192]. The entire state was structured hierarchically in accordance with the Leninist principle of 'democratic centralism', the media was tightly controlled, the rule of law was more honoured in the breach than the observance, there was no separation of powers, and independent societal organizations were heavily proscribed.

To describe the concept of 'SED dictatorship' as 'problematic' because of inefficiencies in the party's administration, as one British historian has done, is untenable [2: 166]. If we are to follow this logic, there has never been a dictatorship in world history, and the famously polycratic Third Reich would certainly not qualify as one – a patent absurdity. The SED dictatorship, for all its shortcomings, was actually one of the most efficient in the twentieth century. Neither does the fact that other parties participated in it change the fact that the SED was its linchpin [2: 166]. The former East German historian, Wilfriede Otto, eschews the word 'dictatorship' in favour of the term 'democracy deficient' [21: 809–10]. Far more convincing is Thomas Lindenberger's observation that 'while as a state the GDR was a dictatorship, not everything that happened on its territory or was meaningful to those who experienced it can be described as "dictatorial"' [125: 5]. Only in the last six months of its life did East Germany become a democracy.

Totalitarian welfare state

But whether or not this dictatorship should be described as 'totalitarian' has always excited great controversy. The fact that totalitarianism theory was sometimes used to denounce the Soviet bloc during the Cold War has no bearing on its academic validity. Totalitarianism is best defined in terms of a ten-point 'syndrome', combining the work of various scholars: an official, all-encompassing and millenarian ideology; a monopolistic political party; 'a terroristic police'; a near-total party monopoly on the mass media; an almost total state monopoly on arms; 'a centrally directed economy' [54: 9–10]; the virtual abolition of civil society [82: 564–5]; pseudo-democracy [100: 15]; state mobilization of the population [126: 70]; and high levels of popular participation in the regime [126: 70]. Notwithstanding the fact that there can be no such thing as an entirely efficient totalitarian polity, East Germany fitted all these criteria. It should be noted here that totalitarianism is not a static but a dynamic concept [138]. Dictatorships can be more or less totalitarian, 'creating a theoretical framework that emphasizes change over time and allows scholars to look for the causes and effects of change' [98: 26].

Heuristically, totalitarianism should be posited not just as a concept but as a theory, on the grounds that it can help *explain* as well as *describe* East German reality. It is treated here, not as an ideal type, but as a really existing historical phenomenon. Totalitarianism may therefore be summarized as 'the concerted but disguised attempt by a state to exercise total control over, coerce, integrate, manipulate, mobilize, and seduce its population in the name of an ideology, regardless of the extent to which this was actually achieved in practice' [82: 565].

The distinguished historian, Tony Judt, observed that 'communism depended upon control – indeed communism *was* control: control of the economy, control of knowledge, control of movement and opinion and people' [103: 597]. In East Germany, this 'control' was taken to extremes, becoming a kind of obsessive-compulsive disorder. The state had to be exalted before everything else, partly because the GDR was an artificial entity and a discrete East German 'nation' did not exist. Ideology, in the guise of Marxist–Leninism and anti-fascism, provided the substitute identity. Only the GDR was fêted as the 'Workers' and Peasants' State' [29: 284]. According to Kopstein, the SED's devotion to ideological instruction helps explain 'why the vast majority of the East German elite remained loyal to the ideas of socialism' and why it avoided 'the kind of spectacular corruption seen in Poland, Hungary, and Romania during the 1970s and 1980s' [114: 128–9].

The GDR was also on the front-line of the Cold War, vulnerable to subversion from the West. This exacerbated the controlling instincts of the regime. Partly because this was a relatively small and technically advanced country with a concentrated population, the SED found it easier to establish the most Orwellian surveillance apparatus in history. One of the party's favourite words was *Maßnahme* or 'measure', the title of a book about its rule published in 1991 [161a]. As John Connelly has discovered, the archetypal grass-roots SED organization held more meetings and adopted more resolutions on more issues than their Czech or Polish equivalents. It also established more sophisticated organizations to accomplish more far-reaching goals. Junior officials incessantly exhorted and lectured those who worked under them. Words like 'control' and 'supervise' feature more frequently and more conspicuously in party documents. In 1950, SED Central Committee Secretary, Ernst Hoffmann, articulated the party's totalitarian impulse with regard to education policy: *'Es darf nichts unkontrolliert bleiben'* ('nothing may escape our control') [29: 285].

Studies that focus on the 'limits' of the East German dictatorship [12; 183] lack historical context because they fail to consider the really existing totalitarianism of other Communist states [29: 285]. GDR totalitarianism was a lot more efficient (or rather a lot *less inefficient*) than that of its Soviet bloc neighbours, even if it ultimately failed to achieve the dystopian levels of control envisaged by the SED. The regime did not just nationalize the means of production, distribution, and exchange; it came closer than any other to nationalizing society. As Eric Hobsbawm has noted, 'In some countries of "real socialism", as for instance Poland, it was possible to avoid the party in one's dealings with colleagues and friends. Not so in the German Democratic Republic where nothing was outside its supervision' [96: 147]. That said, no regime in history has succeeded in abolishing private life. Carl Friedrich and Zbigniew Brzezinski identify 'the family' as the most important 'island of separateness' in the totalitarian sea [54: 239–47]. In a trail-blazing study, Paul Betts has shown that the private sphere assumed a central importance for GDR citizens [13].

According to Eli Rubin, 'the totalitarian school sees only state power and only in hard forms' [191: 9]. Such simplistic and stereotypical interpretations of totalitarianism theory do not necessarily follow from the theorem itself, which is flexible enough to encompass softer, subtler forms of power. Policies pursued by totalitarian states can sometimes be popular with their citizens, either because the regime propagates them successfully or because they fulfil a genuine popular need. Often it is a combination of both. As Charles S. Maier has pointed out, 'there were always projects worthy of support' in totalitarian societies from 'peace campaigns' to 'mobilization against revanchism' and 'educational reforms'. 'East European communism', he perceptively observed, 'was repression tempered by enthusiasms' [133: 53].

Totalitarianism can be 'bottom-up' as well as 'top-down'. In East Germany, people from all walks of life cooperated with the infamous Ministry for State Security (MfS), also known as the Stasi or 'Firm'. The historian Mike Dennis has classed their motives under five general headings: 'political and ideological conviction; coercion and fear; personal advantage; emotional needs; and a desire to influence official policy.' This cooperation was usually determined by a complex variety of motives rather than just one [40: 97]. According to the Stasi's own statistics, only 7.7 per cent of 'unofficial collaborators' (IMs) were recruited by means of unambiguous coercion. Of course, this figure does not take account of more inchoate feelings of fear, guilt or entrapment caused by tactics which might have stopped just short of coercion, such as certain forms of bullying [64: 243]. It is important to note that approximately 'one in three targets approached to be IMs did in fact refuse' [195: 36].

Totalitarian models need not present society as the helpless victim of the state. After all, in totalitarian systems it was civil society, not society itself that was largely 'shut down'. The purpose of a totalitarian state was to control society, not to destroy it [82: 572]. If East German society had 'withered away', as the social scientist Sigrid Meuschel alleges [151: 10], the totalitarian polity would have lost its *raison d'être*. Its failure to do so cannot therefore be used as an argument to deny the latter's existence. Society continued to exist, albeit robbed of its independent voice and most of it was confined within state structures. Precisely because the state incorporated the bulk of society, it was also, to an extent, shaped by it. All systems can be manipulated from below, even totalitarian ones [82: 572]. As Corey Ross points out, ordinary East Germans had their own agendas – often referred to as '*Eigen-Sinn*', or 'a sense of one's interests' – which occasionally coincided and frequently clashed with government policies [188: 8–9]. The 'creative accommodation' or *modus vivendi* that they reached with the regime helped to consolidate it, at least in the short and medium term. To put it another way, ordinary East Germans exercised a degree of agency in this dictatorship. Mary Fulbrook's argument that it is impossible to allot the 'silent majority' of people 'any active voice or historical role' whilst retaining the totalitarianism thesis lacks cogency [62: 618]. Studies which fail to do this can hardly be blamed on the theory itself, which is sufficiently adaptable to take account of the multiple symbiotic links between state and society. If it can be done for the Third Reich [3], then it can be done for East Germany. Needless to say, the fact that the GDR was an out–and–out 'grumble society' [174: 115] does not detract from its totalitarian nature. While the petition system acted as a safety-valve, it also served to atomize protest.

Having said all that, it would be dogmatic to claim that any one theory is capable of capturing all aspects of life in a given society. The concept of a 'welfare state' is therefore integrated to take account of the Socialist paternalism exercised by the SED, particularly from the early 1970s. A 'welfare state' is one that caters for the social needs of its inhabitants. Those of the Communist world provided centralized, compulsory, free, cradle-to-grave cover as a bureaucratic government near-monopoly, often in exchange for tacit ideological and political compliance. Although their main purpose was to *serve* the population, they could also be used to *control* it.

A certain Major Klaus Risse has provided evocative testimony of the symbiotic relationship that sometimes existed between welfare and oppression in the GDR. His father died 'on active service' during the Second World War. The family lost everything they owned in the bombing raids. His mother, an agricultural labourer, kept them alive. Then the East German state began to provide support. Klaus was a promising pupil and the government awarded him the highest scholarship to attend a boarding school. Aged 18, he had to decide on a career. He longed to study fishery at university. But the Stasi said, 'do something for the state which has done so much for you'. So he became an employee of the MfS [70: 172–3]. Thus it came to pass that this impoverished child of the Second World War was emotionally blackmailed into working for one of the most sinister secret police organizations of the twentieth century. Those state benefits he had received as a vulnerable child provided the means for his recruitment. The victim had become a victim again, this time by entering the ranks of the key perpetrators [82: 579].

Care and coercion were closely linked in the minds of the SED leaders. One of the most poignant moments in the collapse of East Germany was the valedictory speech of Erich Mielke, Minister for State Security since 1957, to the country's newly emboldened parliament on 13 November 1989. As deputies began to jeer and heckle, he exclaimed: 'but I love you all, each and every one of you!' (*'aber ich liebe euch doch alle!'*). Even Mielke's most loyal supporters exploded in contemptuous laughter [112: 407; 76: 378; 40: 233]. This was Mielke's moment of truth. The tragedy was that the Stasi chief really did love the people of the GDR and their bogusly elected representatives. He can best be compared to an obsessively authoritarian, over-protective father who wanted to subject his children to total control so that no harm came to them. Consequently, they felt smothered and ended up hating him. That the SED infantilized the East German population can hardly be disputed [190: 31]. After the 1989 Revolution, Mielke said that he had only tried his utmost to protect the 'Workers' and Peasants' Power' from internal and external enemies.

It may be objected that the concept of a 'totalitarian welfare state' is inappropriate because it can just as well be applied to the Third Reich. But totalitarianism is a species, not an individual beast. Many of the other concepts examined below can also be applied to both German dictatorships. To demarcate it clearly from the GDR, Nazi Germany is better characterized as a 'racist-totalitarian welfare state' [3: 2].

A critical analysis of 11 alternative interpretations now follows.

Introduction

'Welfare dictatorship'

One of the most innovative concepts conceived in the past 20 years is that of 'welfare dictatorship' (*'Fürsorgediktatur'*). Konrad Jarausch coined the neologism in 1999 to capture the paradoxical combination of care and coercion in the GDR [98: 47–69]. Other historians such as Alan McDougall and Eli Rubin went on to use it in their own work [147: 13; 191: 37, 84]. While SED leader Erich Honecker expanded the welfare state, it already existed in less developed form under Walter Ulbricht. Andrew Port's contention that the Honecker era was 'the only period in which the GDR could perhaps be accurately characterized as a "welfare dictatorship"' is therefore difficult to sustain [174: 274].

However, the term does present other problems. According to Jarausch, it 'attempts to elucidate the specific nature of the GDR in the context of other modern dictatorships of the twentieth century' [98: 60]. In this it is not very successful. After all, many twentieth-century dictatorships provided some kind of welfare for their citizens. The concept also understates the all-encompassing nature of SED rule. While East Germany's 'security state' was concerned with both social and state security, it placed greater emphasis on the latter. Welfare did not detract from East German totalitarianism; it was partly integrated with it. If the GDR is instead conceptualized as a totalitarian welfare state, it is distinguished more clearly from regimes which might more accurately be described as authoritarian in character.

'Autalitarianism'

According to the political scientist, Juan Linz, authoritarian dictatorships differ from totalitarian ones in that they permit greater political pluralism, provide minimal ideological orientation, and attempt to mobilize their citizens less [100: 15; 126: 159]. Using these criteria, Eckhard Jesse concluded that the GDR had become a hybrid of totalitarianism and authoritarianism by the second half of the 1980s, hence the neologism 'autalitarianism' [100: 23]. Yet his analysis is problematic. Although illegal dissident groups were able to form within the interstices of decrepit totalitarian structures, this hardly amounted to political pluralism in any meaningful sense. Totalitarian states have always had to contend with resistance activity [54: 281–9]. Marxist–Leninist ideology had never been embraced by the majority of East Germans, yet SED leaders continued to proselytize it until late 1989. The SED also continued to mobilize the population, albeit to a lesser extent than under Ulbricht. During the Honecker era, East Germany moved from conservative to sclerotic totalitarianism. As elucidated above, the features of a totalitarian state can fluctuate in importance over time.

'Post-totalitarian party police state'

This label was suggested by Mike Dennis in 2003. The 'party police state' aspect nicely 'underlines the dictatorial nature of SED rule and the fact that, unlike in Poland in the 1980s, the East German secret services remained subject to the overall political and normative control of the Communist Party even though their operational latitude may have been greater than is often believed' [40: 12].

The main problem lies with the prefix 'post-totalitarian', which is supposed to denote 'the less brutal and terroristic form of rule which emerged gradually from the chrysalis of Khrushchev's deStalinization campaigns. In contrast to the Stalinist era, compliance rather than [a] revolutionary dynamic pervaded the system, a limited but highly contested degree of space existed for a parallel society, and the top leaders tended to be more bureaucratic and state-technocratic than charismatic' [40: 11–12]. Yet totalitarianism is predicated on bureaucratic control rather than terror. Once high levels of control have been established, terroristic practices become less frequent. Garton Ash gives credit to George Orwell for seeing that 'the perfect totalitarian system is the one that does not need to kill or physically torture anyone' [68: 337]. Totalitarianism is more than a method of rule; it is a system of government. Dennis himself admits that the term 'post-totalitarian' can be applied only to the later Ulbricht years and the Honecker era, which means that the GDR must have been totalitarian for at least half its history. As for the second half, the same objections apply as with 'autalitarianism' above. In some respects, East Germany became *more* totalitarian during the final two decades of its existence: the economy was recentralized, the role of the state was expanded [220: 160–1], and the Stasi hypertrophied. Klaus Schroeder has attempted to redefine this latter period in terms of 'late totalitarianism' [196: 643, 648].

'Modern dictatorship'

In 1999 Jürgen Kocka coined the term 'modern dictatorship' to describe East Germany. The term 'modern' was supposed to denote its 'bureaucratic administration … the modernity of its repressive measures of control and means of mobilization … the mass party with its claims to absolute control', and the legitimization of these claims through 'a binding and all-encompassing ideology' [98: 21]. These criteria are virtually synonymous with those of totalitarianism theory and therefore offer nothing new.

The concept also begs the question of just how 'modern' the GDR was. It is as well to remember that 'modernity' is an ill-defined, relative and contested term. 'Socialist modern', according to a recent study, 'was precisely the regime's more comprehensive project of social engineering … one that set its sights on the full-scale makeover of the state, society, material culture, and citizens alike' [170: 8]. Again, this sounds very much like totalitarianism. Moreover, East Germany suffered from modernization deficits in a number of areas. Since the eastern part of Germany already had an advanced industrial base in 1945, Soviet-type socialism was not the force for modernity it became elsewhere [190: 40]. In fact, the command economy inhibited the GDR's modernizing potential in the long run.

As Hobsbawm has noted, communism 'set out to transform a specified number of aspects of life – state power, property relations, economic structure and the like', while freezing others 'in their pre-revolutionary shapes, or at any rate protect[ing] them against the universal continuous subversion of change in Capitalist societies' [95: 368]. In other words, communism sought to *conserve* as well as to modernize. The GDR was no exception. Hence there is some truth in the postulation that, while capitalism transformed the face of Western Europe, the East remained trapped in a Communist time warp [82: 582]. All in all, the concept of 'modern dictatorship' poses more questions than it answers.

'Participatory dictatorship'

Particularly illuminating is Mary Fulbrook's notion of 'participatory dictatorship', conceived in 2005 as the interpretative framework for her excellent book, *The People's State: East German Society from Hitler to Honecker* [64]. East Germans participated in the regime for a variety of reasons, some personal, some political. Doing so did not necessarily mean that they believed in state socialism. Fulbrook estimates that between one and two million grown-ups, i.e. approximately eight to 16 per cent of the adult population, served as a significant functionary in one or more of the party and state bodies in the GDR. This was in addition to the 300,000–400,000 'key functionaries', accounting for roughly three per cent of the adult population, 'who played a really important role in the exercise and securing of power' [64: 237]. Numerous others participated simply by joining one of the regime's official organizations or informing for the Stasi. According to Fulbrook, 'it was possible ... to have occupied a position that was simultaneously located in "state" and "society": ... the dichotomy between "state" and "society" simply does not hold up; the battle lines are more complex and difficult to delineate' [64: 236]. Her analysis is undoubtedly correct.

What Fulbrook does not acknowledge, though, is that all totalitarian polities are participatory in character because they rule *through* rather than *over* society. Totalitarianism is the invasion and occupation of society by the state – a state which has itself been hijacked by and subjugated to a political party. Such dictatorships embraced the 'totality' of society, fusing it with party–state structures. No theorist of totalitarianism has ever denied that substantial sections of the population collaborated with or participated in such regimes. Indeed, collaboration and participation were essential prerequisites for a system which, by definition, drew the entire population into its remit [82: 569–70]. As the anti-Communist dissident and future President of Czechoslovakia, Václav Havel, observed in 1978, the crucial 'line of conflict' did not run between rulers and ruled, but rather '*de facto* through each person, for everyone in his or her way' was 'both a victim and a supporter of the system' [90: 53]. He drew attention to the way that every person was, to a greater or lesser degree, implicated in the regime: 'Individuals ... must *live within a lie*. They need not accept the lie. It is enough for them to have accepted their life with it and in it. For by this very fact, individuals confirm the system, fulfil the system, make the system, *are* the system' [90: 45]. Fulbrook's assertion that totalitarianism theory entails adopting 'an essentially dichotomous approach in separating cleanly between repressive, totalitarian "state" and innocent, oppressed "society"' is therefore misplaced [63: 49].

Of course, it might be objected that while all totalitarian dictatorships are participatory, not all participatory dictatorships are totalitarian. Here we come to a second flaw in Fulbrook's concept. She concentrates solely on the 'participatory' aspect of the East German state to the exclusion of its other characteristics. The SED regime cannot be reduced to any one feature, however important. Thirdly, the concept fails to distinguish the GDR from the Third Reich. This is a significant weakness, given Fulbrook's concern to emphasize the differences between the two dictatorships. Hitler's popularity among Germans probably heightened public participation in the National Socialist regime.

From the SED's point of view, the participatory nature of the 'Workers' and Peasants' Power' was partly what made it 'democratic'. One of the party's key slogans was 'work together, plan together and govern together!' (*Arbeite mit, plane mit, regiere mit!*') [64: 257]. Notwithstanding 'the ways in which views and voices from below were often (though not always) taken seriously and listened to by those in positions of power' [64: 258], the involvement of ordinary East Germans did much to strengthen the totalitarian dictatorship. Many felt obligated to take part, others did so voluntarily.

'Consensus dictatorship' ('*Konsensdiktatur*')

In 2009 Martin Sabrow claimed that the GDR was a 'consensus dictatorship' [32: 168–83]. This description can certainly not be applied to the period before 1961, when the Berlin Wall was constructed, or to the years after 1985, when Gorbachev became Soviet leader. The notion that the East German regime was based on any kind of consensus during the popular uprising of June 1953 or the 1989–90 Revolution lacks all credibility. Unlike the Third Reich, which has been conceptualized as a 'consensus state', SED rule never enjoyed mass popular support.

Perhaps it is more accurate to speak, as Thomas Lindenberger has done, of 'an always precarious dictatorship' predicated on 'tacit minimal consensus' [32: 208–22]. According to him, 'in the absence of a majority believing in the legitimacy of the regime, the latter's authority was not based just on the arbitrary application and threat of state violence, but also on a set of "unpolitical" beliefs and norms shared by both sides of the interaction' [32: 212]. In descending order of importance, these beliefs and norms were: peace; prosperity; work; individual security; family life; women's work; public order and security [32: 212–14]. Needless to say, any kind of consensus, tacit or otherwise, served only to strengthen the totalitarian system.

'Consultative authoritarianism'

In 1968 the West German political scientist Peter Christian Ludz wrote a seminal book in which he argued that East Germany no longer practised totalitarianism but a form of 'consultative authoritarianism' [129: 40–2, 126, 185]. His analysis was founded on the SED elite's increased consultation with technocratic experts during the 1960s as the party's First Secretary, Walter Ulbricht, embraced the 'scientific–technological revolution'. These young experts were, in Ludz's view, more pragmatic than those cadres selected for ideological reasons. They were also more managerial and concerned with administering what was now a 'performance-orientated society'. According to Ludz, the technocrats constituted an 'institutionalized counter-elite'. His book, *The Changing Party Elite of East Germany*, quickly went on to become a classic, helping to persuade West German politicians that it was possible to do business with a 'modern' SED leadership. Ludz's hypothesis seemed to support 'convergence theory', which was fashionable in the 1960s. Advocated by Raymond Aron, John Kenneth Galbraith, and Jan Tinbergen, among others, it stipulated that the demands of an industrial society would erode the differences between Capitalist and Socialist systems, causing them to converge towards a common centre.

Unfortunately, however, Ludz's analysis proved to be wishful thinking. Most GDR technocrats were not only fully integrated into the totalitarian regime, they were also its faithful servants. When Erich Honecker took over from Ulbricht as SED First Secretary in

1971, the role of the technocrats was downgraded [114: 111–29]. As the Honecker era progressed, the party elite developed in precisely the opposite way to that predicted by Ludz [161a: 159]. It became less, not more open to new ideas. The GDR sank deep into conservative totalitarianism. Honecker consulted with only a very small coterie of cronies. Towards the end of his 18-year tenure, he virtually ruled the SED alone [161a: 160].

'Niche society'

In 1983 the first head of the Bonn Republic's permanent mission in the GDR, Günter Gaus, published an influential book in which he popularized the notion that East Germany was a 'niche society' [73]. The term refers to a citizenry which had come to terms with the SED regime 'by leading a double life of outward conformity combined with private authenticity' [59: 129]. It was predicated on the idea that ordinary East Germans were politically 'docile' and 'obedient' [59: 130].

The concept is, however, an oversimplification. First, the archives reveal a population that was less conformist and more proactive in blunting the impact of party policies than had been appreciated at the time. Clearly, there was greater conformity among some groups than others [59: 141–2]. Secondly, GDR citizens did not withdraw into niches on the one hand and kowtow to the dictatorship on the other. According to Esther von Richthofen, 'organized cultural activities in the GDR satisfied people's personal interests' [183: 96]. In the field of sport, Molly Wilkinson Johnson has highlighted the willing participation of athletes and enthusiasts, who tried to realize their individual goals and desires through state organizations [102: 10]. Josie McLellan has concluded that East German nudism was both a niche activity and an attempt to gain official recognition [150: 70, 75]. Thirdly, although there were some niches in this inefficient totalitarian system, they were not immune to state intrusion and people could only retreat into them for short periods. There was actually little escape from the ideological reach of the regime. Marxist–Leninist indoctrination began in kindergarten and continued into adult life. The public realm was saturated with SED propaganda and the state even attempted to organize people's leisure activities. While family and private life afforded a degree of protection, this was sometimes more imagined than real. Radio, television, newspapers, even interior design [170: 96–132] brought Communist ideology into people's homes. The full extent of Stasi penetration was only revealed after 1990. Fourthly, it is does not necessarily follow that by occupying niches East Germans had come to terms with the regime. Indeed, they often occupied them 'because they had not come to terms with it'! [100: 22] Giving priority to private interests was a way of coping with the enforced collectivism of the 'Workers' and Peasants' Power'. In other words, the concept of a niche society as propounded by Gaus, fails to capture the complexity of life under state socialism.

'A society ruled all the way through'

In 1994, German social historian Alf Lüdke coined the term *'durchherrschte Gesellschaft'* – a society ruled through and through – to describe the GDR. The concept was further developed by Jürgen Kocka [104: 188–213, 547–53]. It sought to point up ways in which the SED party–state drenched the whole of society while eschewing the controversial word 'totalitarianism'. The attempt to define East Germany in terms of its society rather than its state is potentially fruitful. However, totalitarian polities are also 'societies ruled all the way through'. Kocka's simultaneous insistence that party–state rule did not 'totally mould and determine society' [104: 550] is fully compatible with the notion of inefficient totalitarianism. In 1969, Carl Friedrich wrote: 'While it may be the intent of the totalitarians to achieve total control, they are certainly somewhat disappointed. No such control is actually achieved even within the ranks of their party membership, let alone over the population at large' [55: 134].

The notion of *'durchherrschte Gesellschaft'* is so lacking in clarity that it has been attacked from the opposite direction as well. Klaus Schroeder, a major proponent of the totalitarianism thesis, has argued that it fails to distinguish the GDR from democratic polities which are, in his view, also 'societies ruled all the way through'. As a consequence, 'the decisive difference between rule legitimized by the consent of the majority and rule based on force or ideological claims, can easily be overlooked in the process' [196: 633; 134: 288].

Stalinism

According to the doyen of GDR studies, Hermann Weber, Stalinism existed in both a general and a specific sense. In a general sense, Stalinism was 'a socio-political system' defined by the omnipotence of the Communist Party which, 'with the help of the political police ... directed the whole of public life' [219: 203]. In a specific sense, Stalinism was a form of 'tyranny' characterized by 'bloody purges, uncertainty regarding the law (*Rechtsunsicherheit*), and personality cult' [219: 203]. Some scholars have deployed the concept to describe the SED's transformation into a party modelled on Stalin's Communist Party of the Soviet Union (CPSU) during the late 1940s and early 1950s [136].

Although Stalinism demarcates the GDR clearly from the Third Reich, it is unsatisfactory at a number of levels. On the one hand, left-wing scholars may attribute the failure of the 'Workers' and Peasants' Power' to the 'distortion' of Communist ideology by Stalin, absolving other Soviet leaders, not to mention Marx and Engels, of any blame. On the other hand, right-wing scholars may misapply the concept to depict the GDR as more oppressive than it actually was. After all, Stalinist rule in the Soviet Union was characterized by genocide and systemic violence, features which were absent from East Germany.

Stalinism in the broad sense reads like an incomplete definition of totalitarianism. Neither is it clearly distinguishable from Leninism. The SED's adoption, with some minor alternations, of the Soviet system from the late 1940s is better captured by the terms 'Bolshevization' and 'Sovietization'. Even Weber's specific definition of Stalinism is somewhat problematic. This is because there were no bloody purges or show trials of SED leaders. Although the population was exposed to the dual personality cult of Stalin and Ulbricht, the former ceased to exist after Khrushchev's attack on Stalin in 1956 and Ulbricht's was rather tame by comparison. While the rule of law never pertained in the GDR, 'uncertainty regarding the law' was mitigated over time. In fact, SED rule became rather predictable as the years went by. All in all, Stalinism in the specific sense was a relatively mild affair in the 'Workers' and Peasants' State'. This partly explains why 'deStalinization' there was so limited after 1956. Since Stalinism was by definition excessive, the notion of 'mild Stalinism' could be seen as oxymoronic. None of this is to deny the serious human rights abuses which occurred, first in the Soviet Occupation Zone and then in East Germany. The term 'Stalinism' cannot easily take account of the fact that Communist methods were refined from the early 1960s onwards. Neither does it consider less repressive aspects of socialism which might have been welcomed by the population.

'Russian satrapy'

According to the distinguished German historian, Hans-Ulrich Wehler, the GDR was little more than a 'Russian satrapy'. In 1992 Peter Abrassimov, Soviet ambassador to East Berlin during the 1960s and 1970s, memorably likened it 'to a homunculus that was reared in the Soviet test-tube' [190: 156]. If these assessments are true, it could be argued that the GDR was not a totalitarian state because real power resided in Moscow [210: 35]. However, this would be to ignore the distinction between the 'inner' and the 'outer' Soviet empire. The latter, which included East Germany, enjoyed significantly more autonomy than the former. In other words, the GDR was a semi-sovereign country, not a Soviet Republic. One of the key findings of researchers since the end of the Cold War is that 'the SED leadership acted with more independence and was more willing to risk tensions with Moscow than has often been assumed' [190: 165]. Even when the SED leaders did implement Kremlin policy, this was usually because they agreed with it. Often they were more hard line than their Soviet patrons. East Germany was ultimately dependent on the USSR but not run by it. While Moscow guaranteed its existence, day-to-day power resided in East Berlin. This became truer as the country developed.

Even if the Kremlin did exercise some power on behalf of the GDR, this would hardly alter the latter's totalitarian nature. After all, the USSR was itself a totalitarian state, and Soviet officials helped to ensure the construction and consolidation of totalitarianism in East Germany. KGB advisors, for example, mentored Stasi agents during the early 1950s. The ten features of the 'totalitarianism syndrome' elucidated above were rendered more effective by Soviet tutelage.

Surprisingly, the GDR managed to preserve its German character more successfully than the Federal Republic of Germany (FRG), which underwent Americanization and Europeanization. After 1990 some scholars interpreted it as an extension of the German '*Sonderweg*' ('special path') [190: 157; 111: 34–45]. The traditional German *Obrigkeitsstaat* ('authoritarian state') is supposed to have achieved its grotesque apotheosis in the 'Workers' and Peasants' Power' [82: 582]. Certainly, 'the GDR retained many of the anti-Western and illiberal features' of the Bismarckian, Wilhelmine and Hitlerian polities [190: 157]. Overy even goes so far as to aver that East Germany 'owed much more of its organization and values to the National Socialist system it replaced than to the Soviet one it emulated' [167: 175], a view supported by the philologist Victor Klemperer, who lived under both. On 14 February 1958, the latter was moved to write in his diary: 'The whole ... is ever less distinguishable from Nazi attitudes and methods. Say working class instead of race and both movements are identical' [109: 506].

While these latter two claims are exaggerated, the SED did harness putative Prussian traits such as *Gründlichkeit* ('thoroughness'), hard work and the desire for order to consolidate its dictatorship. Paradoxically, even traditional German anti-communism served to strengthen the totalitarian system, as the state had to exercise particularly tight control over its unwilling subjects to ensure that they remained compliant. The decimation of civil society and the levelling of class differences wreaked by National Socialism inadvertently facilitated the Communists' meteoric rise to power [82: 582]. Stalin's anti-Zionist campaigns of the early 1950s built upon the entrenched anti-Semitism of many GDR citizens. As for the habit of denouncing their fellow-citizens picked up by Germans during the Nazi period, this surely goes some way to explaining why informing for the secret police became so endemic in the 'Workers' and Peasants' State' [82: 582]. One of the tragic legacies of the Third Reich was that a whole generation of children grew up without fathers: quite often it was by posing as the 'substitute father' that the Stasi managed to recruit its younger victims [70: 225]. It was precisely these 'German' aspects that exacerbated the totalitarian nature of the SED regime [82: 582]. The adoption of the Soviet model of socialism enabled this authoritarian political culture to reproduce itself. As Weitz has shown, 'German communism was shaped also by social, ideological, and political factors indigenous to Germany, or, alternately posed, by aspects of transnational developments indigenous to Europe in the era of high

modernity, which received a particular coloration ... in Germany'
[222: 391–2]. Arnulf Baring's assertion that 'socialism in the GDR
was in essence not something that grew in the country itself, but
always remained a derivative of Russian power and the presence of
the Red Army' [190: 156] therefore requires qualification.

This book elucidates the history of East Germany by dividing it
into six phases: conception, 1945–9; construction, 1949–60; consolidation, 1961–71; conservatism, 1971–7; crisis, 1977–89; and collapse, 1989–90. A chapter is devoted to each. In the conclusion,
the reader is offered an overall assessment of the GDR's life and
legacy. The country's development as a totalitarian welfare state is
highlighted throughout.

1 Conception, 1945–9

Stalin and the German question

During the Cold War and after, controversy raged over whether Stalin aimed for a Germany united under communism, a democratic but neutral Germany, or a separate Communist state in the east [134: 26]. Wettig, Raack and Spilker have argued that he countenanced a united Germany only if it was to be controlled by the Communists and their allies [223; 180: 128, 141; 201]. Conversely, the German historian, Wilfried Loth, has claimed that Stalin was prepared to accept a 'bourgeois–democratic' Germany, so long as it was neutral [127; 128]. Most historians now agree that the dictator never originally set out to transform the Soviet Occupation Zone into a separate Socialist republic. According to Naimark, the Soviets did not even pursue a single or clearly defined goal [154: 466]. Ross concurs, observing that 'the picture of Soviet policy that emerges is one of improvisations and contradictions, especially on the part of Stalin himself, whose single most consistent desire was to keep his options open and not commit himself any earlier than absolutely necessary to either a separate Socialist Germany or a unified neutral Germany' [190: 161–2]. Indeed, if one surveys Stalin's policies in the late 1940s and 1950s, they do – on the face of it – seem inconsistent. On the other hand, it is important to remember that Russian Communists had always regarded Germany as the key to the success of world revolution. In the light of this, the idea that Stalin did not know what he wanted for the country strains credibility. It is more plausible to argue that he pursued a long-term, medium-term and minimum agenda [84: 12–13].

Stalin's long-term objective was to transform a reunited Germany into a fully-fledged Communist state. He is reported as having told Bulgarian and Yugoslav leaders in the spring of 1946 'that all of

Germany must be ours, that is, Soviet, Communist' [44: 119]. But since the nation was divided between the four occupation powers, he could advance towards this goal only slowly. In the medium term, therefore, he advocated the creation of a united, 'democratic' and 'peace-loving' German state (to use the Soviet jargon) on the basis of the Potsdam Agreement signed by the Allies on 2 August 1945 [84: 12]. Such a polity was not, as Loth argues, compatible with the Western idea of democracy; instead, it would have constituted a halfway house between 'bourgeois democracy', on the one hand, and Communist-led 'People's Democracy', on the other. Stalin's vision seems to have been of a 'freely elected' left-wing government for the country as a whole, radically implementing the stipulations in the Potsdam Agreement regarding decartelization, demilitarization, and deNazification. These were regarded by the Communists as essential if the sources of war in Germany – monopoly capitalism and the Junker landowners in Prussia – were to be extirpated [84: 12]. Stalin's tool for achieving this so-called democratic and peace-loving Germany was initially the Communist Party of Germany (KPD). On 4 June 1945 he instructed its leaders, Wilhelm Pieck and Walter Ulbricht, to secure the unity of Germany via 'a uniform KPD, a uniform Central Committee, a uniform party of the working people' [205: 277]. All talk of socialism was taboo. But the KPD lacked popular support, so the Socialist Unity Party of Germany (SED) was founded in the Soviet Occupation Zone on 21–22 April 1946. A merger of the Communists and the Social Democrats, it was pledged to pursuing a gradualist 'special German road to socialism' based on parliamentary democracy [84: 8, 9]. There would be no Socialist 'Zero Hour' in eastern Germany. The idea that the right would be allowed to form a government in a unified Germany was anathema to the Kremlin. Thus Smyser's assertion that the Soviet dictator 'was prepared to accept a non-Communist regime there for the immediate future if it was friendly' [198: 68] lacks precision.

Stalin expected Germany to be divided and for this reason he never ruled out the option of turning his zone into a separate Communist state. But partition was his least favoured scenario and something he countenanced only as a provisional solution. During the meeting with Pieck and Ulbricht on 4 June 1945, he told them: 'Perspective – there will be two Germany's, despite the unity of the Allies' [84: 13]. The Soviet Zone was poorly endowed with raw materials and shorn of its eastern territories. Soviet dismantling of factories and railway lines had rendered it even less viable. It was widely believed by contemporaries in the West that the Russians were preparing 'to extract their reparations and then abandon, for all constructive political purposes, the shell of Eastern Germany' [159: 306]. But this was never on the cards. Although socialism in one-third of a country was hardly a promising prospect for Moscow, it was better than no socialism at all. According to Loth, the GDR was 'Stalin's unloved child' [128]. Whether or not this was true, the Soviet dictator had no intention of surrendering it to the Western Allies.

Why did Stalin's long- and medium-term plans for Germany come to nothing? The first reason is the contradiction between his aims and methods. He wanted the left to win competitive all-German elections, yet Soviet troops raped [154: 69–140] and pillaged their way through eastern Germany. Although intended as a means of rebuilding the USSR, the campaign of economic dismantling alienated the German population and undermined support for the SED. Repression [22: 21–118] and creeping Bolshevization damaged the SED's electoral prospects still further. Stalin grievously misjudged the western German population, believing it to be so nationalistic that it would be seduced by Soviet offers to reunify the Fatherland. In fact, western Germans were far more anti-Communist than nationalist. German nationalism had been discredited by the total defeat of 1945 [172: 1282], whereas anti-communism was given a huge boost by the Cold War and Soviet actions in Eastern Europe.

A key example of Stalin's methods' undermining his objectives was his blockade of all roads, canals, and railway lines leading to West Berlin between 18 June 1948 and 12 May 1949. Historians still disagree about whether he regarded Berlin 'as a lever or a prize' [39: 45]. The answer is probably both. Partly intended to coerce the Western Powers into abandoning plans to establish their own currency, the Blockade ended up deepening Western suspicions and expediting the establishment of a West German state. Stalin also hoped to force the Western Allies to leave Berlin. On 26 March 1949 he told Pieck, 'Let's try with all our might and maybe we'll drive them out' [39: 45]. Whichever objective was more important, neither was achieved. The Americans and British organized the famous Berlin Airlift, which supplied the western sectors of the city and enabled them to survive, causing the USSR to abandon the Blockade after 11 months.

The second reason for the failure of Stalin's long- and medium-term agenda was that the United States decided to divide Germany [46]. Clearly, the Western Allies had more to gain from the partition of the country than the Soviets. Lewkowicz contends that ideology served merely to support the national self-interests of the two Superpowers, which were directed towards a 'spheres of influence policy' [124: 10–11, 79–80, 141–2]. It would be more accurate to say that both sides perceived their security interests through ideologically-tinted spectacles. Hence Stalin imposed 'People's Democracy' on Eastern Europe, hoping to extend it westwards when the opportunity arose. Former Soviet Foreign Minister, Vyacheslav Molotov, testified 'that it had been his task to "expand Soviet frontiers as far as possible" and that there could be no "peace-loving" Germany that was not on "the path to socialism"' [198: 69]. This prompted the Western Powers to transform their part of Germany into a bulwark against Bolshevism. Needless to say, they also wanted to extend capitalism eastwards. The Marshall Plan, implemented in Western Europe but offered to Eastern Europe too, was one way of doing this.

On 7 October 1949, the German Democratic Republic (GDR) was born, four-and-a-half months *after* the Federal Republic of Germany (FRG) was founded in the West. It was the KPD's failure to win more than 5.7 per cent of the popular vote in the first elections to the West German parliament in August that ultimately convinced Stalin to act, although some of the groundwork had already been laid at a meeting with SED leaders in December 1948 [146: 65]. The West refused to recognize the GDR, putting inverted commas around the name or simply referring to the fledgling country as 'the zone' until the late 1960s. Stalin, on the other hand, sent a congratulatory telegram in which he described the new state as a 'turning-point in the history of Europe' [127: 95]. In his view, it was a staging post on the road to a 'united, independent, democratic, peace-loving Germany' [128: 161]. Needless to say, the Communist interpretation of the terms 'independent', 'democratic', and 'peace-loving' contradicted the Western one and, in order to win over as many Germans as possible, the word 'socialism' was not even mentioned.

The formation of the Socialist Unity Party of Germany (SED)

On 21–22 April 1946, 680,000 members of the Social Democratic Party of Germany (SPD) and 600,000 members of the Communist Party of Germany (KPD) merged to form the Socialist Unity Party of Germany (SED) in the Soviet Occupation Zone. This unleashed an intense historical debate which outlasted the Cold War. Many historians in the West characterized it as a 'forced union' (*'Zwangsvereinigung'*) imposed on the SPD by the Soviets and their KPD stooges [173: 319–38; 53: 28]. In the GDR, on the other hand, it was always maintained that the SED had been a voluntary merger between the two parties [7: 58–64]. Another current in Western historiography, represented by Weber and Stuby, argued that it had been something between the two [221: 120–1; 176: 109]. Even so, Weber still leaned heavily towards the 'forced marriage' thesis [219: 27–38]. Only in West Berlin were Social Democrats allowed to vote on the issue. A ballot was held there on 31 March 1946, and of those who participated, 82 per cent rejected the merger [220: 23–4].

With the opening of the East German archives in the 1990s, it finally became possible to shed some light on the controversy. The formation of the SED was neither a 'shotgun wedding' nor a romantic one. Rather it was a marriage arranged by the Soviets, with some consent from both parties. That said, Communists were generally much more enthusiastic than their SPD counterparts, many of whom felt 'tickled by Russian bayonets', to use a phrase attributed to Otto Grotewohl, leader of the SPD in the Soviet Occupation Zone [84: 17]. Most Social Democrats were not ill-disposed to unity in principle because they blamed divisions on the left for facilitating the rise of Hitler. However, they suspected the Communists' motives and wanted to proceed at a slower pace. The SPD had been rebuffed by the KPD when they strongly advocated 'working-class unity' in the first few weeks after the war. Now the latter were campaigning for unification with all the zeal of the recently converted. Although 52.3 per cent of SED members were initially former Social Democrats [53: 30], the arranged marriage of 21–22 April 1946 soon became an abusive and dysfunctional one dominated by the Communists.

Bolshevization

The reasons for the creeping Sovietization of eastern Germany after 1945 are disputed by historians. According to Naimark, 'Soviet officers Bolshevized the zone not because there was a plan to do so, but because that was the only way they knew to organize society' [154: 467]. This is only partly true. There was indeed no Soviet plan to Bolshevize the zone in 1945. Consequently, however, the SED leadership enjoyed more agency than Cold War accounts allow. The prime instigator of Sovietization turned out to be Walter Ulbricht, supported by SMAD hawks such as Sergei Tulpanov. Hurwitz and Malycha argue that the so-called Stalinization of the SED in 1948 actually started two years earlier [97; 136; 137].

Stalin, in the view of Weitz, 'required a loyal party within Germany, but not necessarily a Soviet-style social transformation'. He therefore 'pushed actively for the transformation of the SED into a Soviet-style party, but not for the transformation of Germany into a Soviet-style society' [222: 347]. This latter objective could be pursued only once Germany had been reunited under left-wing auspices. When SED leaders Ulbricht, Pieck, Grotewohl and Fred Oelßner met Stalin in Moscow on 18 December 1948, they came with proposals to turn the Soviet Occupation Zone into a 'People's Democracy'. Pieck recorded Stalin telling them: 'Not yet a unified state – not about to take power' [128: 146]. Ulbricht's push for Sovietization made the foundation of the GDR more likely. While he was bent on consolidating his own influence and building a separate East German state, Stalin wanted to advance more slowly so as not to jeopardize his all-German ambitions. For this reason, the CPSU never permitted the SED to join the Cominform, founded in 1947 as an information bureau of European Communist Parties. Smyser is right that 'Stalin may have made his biggest mistake when he picked Walter Ulbricht as his man in Berlin' [198: 69].

In the second half of 1948 the SED transformed itself into a Bolshevik 'party of the new type'. This meant repudiating the 'special German road to socialism' proclaimed in February 1946. Historians have long debated whether this doctrine ever represented a genuine, viable alternative to the totalitarian dispensation imposed after 1949 [203: 15–31]. To quote its author, Anton Ackermann: 'If the new democratic state develops as a new instrument of power in the hands of reactionary forces, then the peaceful transition to socialism cannot take place. If, however, the anti-fascist democratic Republic becomes a state of all working people under the leadership of the working class, then the peaceful road to socialism is certainly possible, insofar as the use of force against the (completely lawful and legitimate) claim of the working class to all power is impossible' [84: 10]. Ackermann believed that the military defeat of the Third Reich had decimated the reactionary state apparatus, making a Socialist democracy, as opposed to a 'dictatorship of the proletariat', more likely.

The 'special German road' was predicated on the absolute certainty of the SED's winning competitive elections. Yet the precondition of any democracy is the willingness of political parties to concede defeat at the polls, something the Communists were not prepared to do. Thus the 'special German road' was primarily a means of attaining power. It was also instrumental in facilitating the merger of the SPD and the KPD. Having said that, Communists such as Ackermann, and a good many more Social Democrats, sincerely hoped it would inaugurate a more democratic kind of socialism than that pertaining in the USSR [123: 518–21]. As Ackermann told a meeting of the SED Party Executive in October 1946: 'In Germany the possibilities not only of coming to power but also of exercising that power through democratic means are incomparably better than they were in Russia' [84: 11]. For Communist hardliners such as Ulbricht, however, the doctrine represented nothing more than a parliamentary road to Sovietization. Already in 1945, he reportedly told close comrades: 'Things must look democratic but we must have everything in our hands' [123: 440]. According to Weitz, 'two political orientations coexisted in uneasy tension within the KPD and the SED' until the fall of 1948: 'the politics of intransigence' and 'the politics of gradualism'. In the end, the former triumphed over the latter [222: 312]. On 24 September of that year, Ackermann reluctantly engaged in self-criticism [84: 16].

It is sometimes argued that socialism in eastern Germany was predestined to be dictatorial after 1945. The democratic tradition is said to have been too weak, the anti-Communist tradition too strong, the population too infected by Nazism. However, it is worth remembering that the fledgling SED won 47.5 per cent of the popular vote in semi-free elections to the Soviet Zone's regional and district parliaments on 20 October 1946. In Berlin, however, it gained only 19.8 per cent [220: 286]. Of course, by this time the SPD had ceased to exist in the Soviet Zone and other political parties were being disadvantaged by the SMAD. However, there can be little doubt that the SED really did chalk up the most votes. At this point we need to distinguish between Social Democracy and Marxist-Leninism. After the fiasco of Nazism, there was considerable support for some kind of democratic socialism across all four zones of Germany, even among former members of the NSDAP. It should not be forgotten that most of the strongholds of Social Democracy had been in eastern Germany before 1933. The SED, then, was initially quite popular because it had subsumed the SPD, the democratic party of the left.

Contrary to the claims of Hurwitz and Malycha [97; 137], there existed a fleeting chance of a middle way between Bolshevism and Capitalist democracy in 1945 [222: 314, 353–4]. But the opportunity was squandered by the Soviet occupation authorities and their German helpers. The SED's support base declined precipitously once it became perceived as the 'Russian party'. Already on 3 August 1947, Victor Klemperer noted in his diary, 'I am convinced, that in a truly free election today the SED would become a tiny minority party' [109: 211]. This collapse in electoral support prompted its leaders to abandon the 'special German road to socialism'. As the Cold War got underway, Stalin consolidated his grip on Eastern Europe. In the wake of Yugoslavia's expulsion from the Cominform on 28 June 1948, the region's Communist Parties were purged and restructured along Soviet lines. If competitive elections could not keep the Communists in power, then dictatorship was the only option. The SED's metamorphosis into a Bolshevik-type outfit after 1948 only undermined its credibility still further.

By the autumn of 1948, with the SED's campaign against Social Democracy gaining momentum, it was more dangerous in the Soviet Occupation Zone to be a former member of the SPD than an ex-Nazi [84: 19]. In his farewell letter to the SED on 28 October, the former Social Democrat member of the SED leadership, Erich W. Gniffke, wrote: 'today I resign from the "party of the new type", or rather from Ulbricht's KPD of 1932' [77a: 369]. Stibbe estimates that between the summer of 1948 and the end of March 1949, 'around 5,000 ex-Social Democrats were arrested by the Soviet occupation authorities, over 400 of whom died in NKVD/MVD-run prisons in Germany or in forced labour camps in Siberia' [146: 60].

Unlike the SED, the process of Bolshevizing east German society was still in its early stages as the decade ended. With the nationalization of banks and various industries, capitalism was restricted but not abolished. The German Economics Commission, conceived in 1947, was a mere embryo of a planned economy. In September 1945 all landowners with more than 100 hectares had their land expropriated and given to new, private farmers [220: 34]. This radical reform had nothing to do with Soviet-style collectivization and was supported by all the political parties. The SED referred to the years between the end of the war and the foundation of the GDR as the 'anti-fascist–democratic period'. As Nettl observed, 'the process of change went less far in Germany, and was less severely enforced, than in other Communist countries' [159: 311].

Popular opinion

That there was resistance in the Soviet Occupation Zone is not disputed [53]. However, a reader of Gary Bruce's *Resistance with the People* [22] would be forgiven for thinking that the majority of east Germans were politicized by repression and bent on overthrowing the incipient Socialist dictatorship. In fact, they were engaged in a day-to-day struggle for survival and had little, if any, time for politics. Most probably they would have supported any system that provided them with the food and shelter they so desperately needed. Resistance, defined as 'acts, organized or not, which arose from a conscious, political motive, aimed at undermining the political system in some way and bound with a certain degree of risk' [22: 12], was usually futile and counter-productive. The oppression meted out by the authorities was therefore more likely to beget apathy, conformity and despair [83a: 150].

When the GDR was founded, many of its new citizens either did not take any notice or 'adopted a wait-and-see attitude' [2: 49, 50–1; 201: 194]. Some preferred to flee to the West – a relatively easy thing to do in the late 1940s. The availability of this option, together with the fact that Germany was a broken, defeated, and occupied country, explains why there was so *little* resistance to the emerging totalitarian regime in the east [83a: 150]. In 1949 alone, '125,245 people fled the Soviet Occupation Zone/GDR' to go and live in western Germany/the FRG [220: 289]. That is not to say that East Germany's inhabitants were bereft of all agency. As the historian Paul Steege has so expertly demonstrated, the citizens of Berlin played an important role in making possible that city's iconic Cold War status [206].

Although many East Germans bitterly resented the abuses of the Soviet occupiers and their SED counterparts, this did not necessarily make them convinced democrats, as Bruce claims. Most Germans had *never* believed in democracy and any faith they might once have had in it was further undermined by the ignominious failure of the Weimar Republic. Democratic structures in the western zones were in the incubation stage, so their magnetic pull was still weak. Another of Bruce's arguments is that a basic harmony existed between the aims and motives of resisters in the bourgeois parties and those in the wider population. This is certainly true up to a point. During the early post-war years, the ranks of the Christian Democratic Union (CDU) and the Liberal Democratic Party of Germany (LDPD) were swelled with people who wanted to see Germany made safe for capitalism, albeit of a reformed variety. But only a minority of these engaged in resistance. Both the CDU and the LDPD were gradually purged and turned into appendages of the SED. This caused them to become ever less representative of the population. The real story of the bourgeois parties is their collaboration with the emerging totalitarian order [83a: 151].

Of course, there were some genuine supporters of the Soviet occupation. Nettl sorts them into three categories. Firstly, Communists and former Social Democrats who were now loyal to the SED. Second, 'the opportunists who made a career in the Eastern zone by subscribing to the politics of those in power'. Thirdly, 'those who received real personal advantages, the ex-workers now promoted to managerial posts in the nationalized industries, refugees from Eastern Europe who received land and property for their support, a small number of landless agricultural labourers who became small farmers and liked it' [159: 313].

'*Resistenz*' – a scholarly concept conceived by Martin Broszat to analyse the National Socialist period, meaning 'effective warding off, delimitation, containment of the … regime or its claims, irrespective of who or which forces were involved or from what motives' [81: 241] – proved more effective than *resistance* in lessening the impact of Sovietization. Examples of '*Resistenz*' included pre-existing 'social networks and ways of life' in rural communities; the strong influence of the churches in many places [188: 205]; large-scale depoliticization following the traumas of the Weimar and Nazi years; and what Nettl calls 'the obstinate middle-class nature of German society' [159: 311–12]. According to Pritchard, the German tradition of socialism both obstructed and facilitated so-called Stalinization [176: 227–8]. In this context, it is worth remembering that Sovietization did not always clash with indigenous customs.

2 Construction, 1949–60

Pseudo-democracy, purges, and persecution

East Germany's first constitution, promulgated when the GDR was founded on 7 October 1949, differed little from that of the Weimar Republic and other 'bourgeois democracies'. Yet pseudo-democracy is a defining characteristic of totalitarian regimes. It manifested itself in the first (delayed) elections to the GDR's national, regional, local, and communal parliaments held on 15 October 1950. According to Communist propaganda, they were the most democratic ever held in Germany [84: 63]. In reality, they were uncompetitive in nature and the distribution of seats had been decided in advance. Voters were asked to endorse or reject single lists of candidates comprising members from all the political parties and mass organizations. The lists were drawn up by the Communist-controlled National Front. The proposed candidates could only be confirmed, not chosen at election meetings [122: 71]. Many bourgeois party nominees were Communist stooges. As for those from the mass organizations, most were allied to the SED, giving this party an absolute majority. Voters were expressly forbidden to reject some candidates on the lists and support others. Very few dared to vote 'no' to the lists in their entirety.

The polls were conducted in a climate of fear, deliberately whipped up by the Communists. Purges of all parties had been carried out shortly beforehand and a campaign of so-called vigilance launched. To demonstrate their loyalty to the regime, voters were expected to endorse the National Front lists [122: 69–70]. However, fear was only one side of the equation: bribery was the other. A few weeks before the elections, new laws were passed, providing credit for small farmers and financial assistance for the incapacitated. At the same time it was made abundantly clear, even in parliament, that the beneficiaries had the duty to say thank you by voting 'yes' on 15 October [122: 71]. Thus a link had been established between totalitarianism, on the one hand, and welfare, on the other.

According to the official figures, 99.7 per cent of the electorate voted 'yes' and turnout was registered at 87.44 per cent [220: 290]. In violation of the constitution, the ballot 'was conducted openly rather than secretly in many places' [220: 45]. Subsequent GDR elections would follow the same pattern. Otto Grotewohl became the country's first Prime Minister, a position subordinate to that of SED General Secretary. Ulbricht had been elected to the latter post at the party's First Central Committee Plenum on 25 July. The *Volkskammer* ('People's Chamber') quickly atrophied into an acclamation and declamation body, rubber-stamping laws drawn up by the SED Politburo.

On 8 February 1950, the Ministry for State Security (or Stasi) was born. Regarding itself as the 'shield and sword' of the party, its precise role and functions were never properly defined in GDR law. The MfS's full-time workforce grew rapidly from approximately 1,100 in 1950 to 8,800 two years later and it accumulated ever more powers [40: 27]. Almost immediately after it was founded, the Stasi began persecuting its fellow-citizens, including members of the SED.

A number of purges and show trials took place lower down the system between 1950 and 1953. In the paranoid atmosphere of the early Cold War, significant numbers of so-called Western émigrés (those who had spent the Second World War in the West) were demoted or expelled from the party, on the grounds that they were contaminated by 'imperialist ideology'. That is not to say, however, that they were necessarily less Stalinist in their attitudes than those who had emigrated to the Soviet Union. Those who had come into contact with Noel Field, an American Communist falsely accused of working for the CIA, were particularly vulnerable. Field was the key witness in the major East European show trials staged in Hungary and Czechoslovakia. Other veteran Communists, who seemed just as likely to be purged, were unaffected. As Catherine Epstein has observed, the purges were 'arbitrary and irrational' in many respects [47: 153].

A striking characteristic of this wave of persecution in the GDR was anti-Semitism, this time in the guise of anti-Zionism and 'anti-cosmopolitanism' [92: 106–61]. In the East German translation of the collected works of Stalin, Zionism was defined as 'a reactionary nationalistic movement that had its followers among the Jewish bourgeoisie, the intellectual elite and the backward strata of the Jewish mass of workers' [20: 214]. Its protagonists were accused of aiming 'for the isolation of the Jewish mass of workers from the collective struggle of the proletariat' [20: 214]. Anti-cosmopolitanism featured strongly in the propaganda of the SED in the early 1950s, despite having formerly been a staple ingredient of German nationalism, the traditional preserve of the right [151: 16]. According to the SED Central Committee member, Ernst Hoffmann, cosmopolitanism was 'the ideal of the "money man"', a 'man without a country'. This man's bourgeois worldview symbolized 'the most complete image of Capitalist exploitation' [92: 111–12]. In 1893 the German Social Democrat, August Bebel, had defined anti-Semitism as 'the socialism of fools' [92: 46]. He could not have known that one day the 'fools' would seize power, first as National Socialists, then as Communists.

Paul O'Doherty downplays the importance of anti-Semitism, arguing that '"Zionism" was a "convenient" if insensitive additional charge levelled against defendants who happened to be of Jewish origin' [164: 302, 317]. According to Keβler and Klein, the SED's policy towards East Germany's tiny population of Jews was 'largely determined by the Soviet Union' [98: 118]. Yet while the USSR set the tone, Ulbricht was happy to play the anti-Zionist card against his political opponents. By concocting a brew of patriotism with anti-Semitic and anti-Capitalist ingredients, the SED hoped 'to combine the right- and left-wing critique of Western Capitalist societies' and thereby boost its own position [151: 112]. It was also an effective way of integrating former Nazis into the 'anti-fascist order'.

Communist doctrine stipulated 'that Jews and Judaism would wither away in a classless society' [92: 131]. In early 1953, Hans Jendretzky, a candidate member of the SED Politburo and full member of its Central Committee, called for Jews to be banned from public life, branding them 'enemies of the state' [92: 132–3]. According to Meuschel, the flats of Jewish tenants 'were routinely searched, their papers and identity cards seized. The leaders of the Jewish community were interrogated and ... required to equate Zionism with fascism'. Moreover, they had 'to refuse compensation payments on the grounds that they amounted to exploitation of the German people. In early 1953, rabbis and heads of Jewish communities called on the Jewish inhabitants of the GDR to leave the country' [151: 114]. By 30 March of that year around one-third had done so [60: 58]. According to Thomaneck and Niven, 'their numbers dwindled from 5,000 to between 300 and 400 by the end of the 1980s' [212: 83]. On 21 February 1953, as Meuschel points out, 'the SED dissolved the VVN ("The Association of Those Persecuted by the Nazi Regime") and replaced it with "The Committee of Anti-fascist Resistance Fighters"', in which the Nazi persecution of the Jews could not be discussed [151: 114].

During the early 1950s, preparations were under way in East Germany to stage a major show trial of top Communist leaders, similar to those in Hungary, Bulgaria, and Czechoslovakia. The main defendants were to be ex-Politburo members Paul Merker and Franz Dahlem. The former had spent the Second World War in France and Mexico; the latter had been interned in a French concentration camp at Vernet until 1942. Although not himself Jewish, Merker had used his position during the war to defend the Jewish people. Afterwards he supported the state of Israel [92: 98–100]. All this was proof enough to his interrogators that he was an 'imperialist agent' [84: 30]. Another key defendant was to be the KPD politician and West German Member of Parliament, Kurt Müller, who had been apprehended in East Berlin in March 1950 [146: 75, n67].

There are seven possible reasons why this elite show trial did not in the end take place. First, Stalin's determination to keep the 'German question' open [205: 276, 289] prompted him to delay the charade in order to win popular support in the West. Perhaps he also needed to keep former leaders such as Dahlem and Merker alive in case Ulbricht and his supporters proved a liability in all-German elections. Second, the GDR still had an open border with the Federal Republic and West Berlin, enabling Western journalists to infiltrate the country and prospective victims to flee it. Third, the East German President, Wilhelm Pieck, seems to have afforded some protection to Merker [84: 30–1]. Fourth, there was a marked relaxation in Soviet domestic and foreign policy following the death of Stalin on 5 March 1953. Fifth, at the Kremlin's behest, a liberal 'New Course' was proclaimed in the GDR in the spring of that year. Sixth, the Soviet Interior Minister, Lavrenti Beria, whose agents had organized much of the persecution across East–Central Europe, was arrested on 26 June 1953 and executed a few months later. Seventh, Merker and Dahlem refused to cooperate with attempts to frame them as 'imperialist agents' [84: 216].

Until recently the most popular explanation for the failure of this show trial to materialize was an alleged lack of 'appetite' on the part of the SED. Yet the evidence indicates otherwise [146: 68–70]. Ulbricht cooperated with the trial preparations [84: 29; 50: 230, 232]. Moreover, it was the SED's Central Party Control Commission, responsible for internal discipline, that purged the party of 'hostile and degenerate elements' [98: 114]. The witch-hunt psychology gripped all Politburo members [84: 36]. After 1954, the GDR held a succession of secret trials which handed down severe sentences [98: 115]. Merker was brought before the Supreme Court in 1955 and condemned to eight years' imprisonment. In truly Orwellian fashion, he was found guilty of 'war mongering and incitement to racial hatred' [84: 30]. The fact that this happened after the death of Stalin and Beria shows that Stalinism in the GDR had put down native roots [92: 158]. O'Doherty's argument that these two men orchestrated both the purges and show trial preparations is therefore one-sided [164: 311, 317]. Much more convincing is the thesis advanced by Epstein: 'Although Soviet authorities initiated these purges, SED officials not only cooperated with their Soviet counterparts, but also pursued their own lines of investigation. Moreover, Walter Ulbricht and other members of the SED leadership benefited from these investigations: they removed uncomfortable rivals, they subjected influential veteran Communists to party discipline, and they were able to explain GDR economic and other shortcomings by pointing to a vast conspiracy bent on undermining East German socialism' [47: 154].

The 'Stalin Note'

On 10 March 1952, Stalin sent a 'note' to the Western Powers in which he offered to sign a peace treaty with a reunited Germany. While the country would be permitted her own defence forces, she would be prohibited from joining military alliances against those powers which had defeated her in the Second World War. The stated aim was to create conditions 'conducive to the development of Germany as a united, independent, democratic and peace-loving state in accordance with the Potsdam decisions' [84: 63]. As Spilker observes, the initial draft, which did not differ in its fundamentals from the definitive version, emphasized that the GDR's 'democratic transformation' – code language for the Communist restructuring of the economy – would have to be extended to the FRG if reunification were to occur. This requirement did not appear in the final Soviet offer, implying that it was withheld for 'tactical' reasons and would be brought up again later [201: 230]. Other stumbling blocks included a ban on parties and organizations 'hostile to peace and democracy' (open to broad interpretation) and a commitment to the Oder–Neisse Line as the country's eastern border. Western governments responded by demanding all-German free elections as a prerequisite for a peace treaty and German unity. Stalin then issued a second note on 9 April 1952, in which he declared himself in favour of such elections [84: 63].

The so-called Stalin Note has always excited great controversy. On the one hand, Loth maintains that the West missed a historic opportunity to reunify Germany as a democratic and non-Socialist state [128: 184]. On the other, Wettig and Spilker argue that the note was an attempt by Stalin to expand his influence into the Federal Republic [223: 205–34; 201: 226–32]. According to them, the Soviet dictator was not interested in serious compromise with the West. To quote Spilker again: 'On balance, it would seem that the Stalin Note was just another attempt by the Kremlin to extend a left-wing and pro-Soviet regime across the whole of Germany. Although the note was underpinned by a realization that this regime would differ from the one set up in the GDR, since it would include a larger number of non-Communists, there is no evidence to suggest that the Kremlin would have settled for a bourgeois democratic Germany even on the basis of formal neutrality' [201: 231]. Hermann Graml has characterized the initiative as nothing more than a propaganda stunt [127: 158]. Soviet Foreign Ministry documents can be used to support all three interpretations.

Heike Amos and Michael Lemke have shown that during this period the SED did not see any contradiction between national unity and socialism [4: 336; 121]. This suggests that Soviet–GDR proposals on German reunification were more than mere propaganda stunts. Stalin's note seems to have been prompted by the imminent integration of the Bonn Republic into an anti-Communist military alliance (the proposed European Defence Community) in 1952. Terrified of German militarism after two invasions of his homeland since the beginning of the century, Stalin was determined to prevent this from happening. He also wanted to advance the cause of socialism in Germany as a whole. In his view, this was the only way of guaranteeing peace. Stalin clearly did not intend negotiating with the conservative government of Konrad Adenauer in Bonn, which he depicted as a 'dictatorship of the imperialist German bourgeoisie' and an American puppet regime. Instead, he hoped to galvanize the Left and other pro-unification forces in the Federal Republic to elect a new government willing to treat with the Soviets. At the minimum, Stalin could divide his opponents, win a spectacular propaganda victory and increase support for the Communists by posing as the champion of German unity. At the maximum, Stalin hoped to achieve his medium-term objective of a united, 'democratic' and 'peace-loving' Germany with draconian restrictions on monopoly capitalism [84: 63–4]. The state he envisaged would not have been an exact replica of the GDR and for this reason some East German leaders were nervous [84: 65]. Initially at least, the SED would have had to share power with the SPD. Only later would the entire country have been propelled towards Soviet-style communism.

Stalin's promise to hold 'free elections' should be regarded with the utmost scepticism; by 1952 the Communists no longer felt confident of winning a competitive contest, so it was hardly surprising that Stalin rejected Western demands for United Nations' election monitors. This ensured that the elections in the GDR would be run by the SED, allowing the party to inflate its support artificially by mobilizing the mass organizations under its tutelage. Single lists of candidates on the 1950 model would have secured another victory for the East German regime [84: 63].

As Stalin expected, the Western Powers rejected his offer. Two days before he despatched his second note, the Soviet dictator had told the SED leadership to 'organize [its] own state' and begin building an East German army. Meeting Pieck, Ulbricht, and Grotewohl on 7 April 1952, he is on record as having said: 'Irrespective of any proposals that we can make on the German question the Western Powers will not agree with them. … It would be a mistake to think that a compromise might emerge or that the Americans will agree with the draft of a peace treaty … the Americans need their army in West Germany to hold Western Europe in their hands' [84: 64].

On 8 May it was announced that the GDR would acquire national armed forces [220: 292]. Stalin then allowed Ulbricht to proclaim the 'accelerated construction of socialism' at the SED's Second Conference between 9 and 12 July 1952. However, he agreed to the new policy only one day before the conference started. In his telegram to the delegates, he eschewed the term 'socialism' altogether and confined himself to wishing the SED 'new successes' in the 'historical task of creating a united, independent, democratic and peace-loving Germany'. Soviet officials broke with tradition and stayed away from the proceedings [84: 59]. Neither did Stalin mention the word 'socialism' in his congratulatory telegram to mark the third anniversary of the GDR [84: 64].

The Uprising of 17 June 1953

The 'accelerated construction of socialism' entailed launching a campaign against private businesses, forcing the pace of collectivization in the countryside and prioritizing heavy industry over the production of consumer goods. Reparations and Soviet-decreed militarization placed an additional burden on the East German economy. This was paid for by increased exports to the USSR, higher taxes, and cuts in welfare [59: 179]. In the political sphere, government became even more centralized when the five states (*Länder*) were replaced with 14 districts (*Bezirke*), each under the control of a regional chief secretary. The holder of this office was always a member of the SED [145: 40]. Political trials and purges proliferated and tighter control was exercised over the bourgeois parties. Religious education was banned in schools and the Protestant youth groups or *Junge Gemeinden* ('young congregations') were prohibited. Artists were required to conform to the doctrine of 'Socialist realism' and attempts were made to impose 'the leading role of the SED' on educational establishments. The legal system became a weapon in the class struggle [145: 39–40]. This crash course in Sovietization triggered an economic crisis, exacerbated the refugee outflow, and deepened divisions with the West. According to Volker Koop, living standards in 1952 fell below 1947 levels [113: 41].

In early June 1953 the Kremlin ordered the SED leadership to instigate a New Course, effectively reversing the previous policy. All propaganda about the building of socialism in the GDR was suspended and the creation of a 'united, democratic, peace-loving and independent Germany' became the top priority [84: 68]. However, this abrupt U-turn unleashed the violent disturbances of 17 June 1953, confirming Alexis de Tocqueville's observation 'that the most critical moment for bad governments is the one which witnesses their first steps toward reform'* [84: 53]. In some places enraged crowds ransacked buildings belonging to the SED and mass organizations before setting them ablaze. In others they tried to storm prisons and release political prisoners [145: 44]. Police stations, court houses and offices of the Stasi were also attacked [145: 38; 200: 630]. It was the first popular revolt in the Eastern bloc. A state of emergency had to be declared and the serious unrest quelled by Soviet tanks. The death toll, although still unclear, is now believed to have been 'much lower than the several hundred reported by some Western sources during the Cold War era' [145: 45]. This was partly because the Soviet military showed restraint and partly because a majority of the demonstrators melted away peacefully [145: 45; 200: 638].

There are four interrelated debates concerning this seminal event in East German history. First, did it constitute an uprising [10; 42; 87], a 'revolutionary uprising' [152], or a revolution [22; 200]? Second, was it overwhelmingly working-class in character [10; 42; 220; 204; 215] or should the appellation 'people's uprising' be adopted; that is to say, were other social groups significantly involved? [116; 87; 22; 152; 43; 113; 225; 145: 48; 35: 188]. Third, was it fuelled primarily by economic [10] or political grievances [22]? Fourth, what did the strikers and demonstrators actually want?

If revolution is defined as the implosion or overthrow of a political and social system, then what occurred in the GDR on 17 June does not merit the description. Although the Communist edifice came perilously close to collapse, the Soviet army intervened to prevent that from happening. Troops swiftly restored order and quelled the uprising. In Görlitz, an alternative democratic administration was constituted, with the re-foundation of the SPD and proposals for the election of a municipal council [59: 185; 145: 53, n.30]. In Halle-Merseburg and Magdeburg, strike committees of workers temporarily seized control [220: 48]. But these were the exceptions, not the rule. The 17 June 1953 rebellion in East Germany did not spawn any national revolutionary organizations. This is in marked contrast to the autumn of 1989, when the SED dictatorship was in its death throes and countrywide opposition groups quickly coalesced [83a: 152].

Historians differ as to the extent of the uprising. According to Pritchard, 'of the 18 million inhabitants of the GDR at that time, fewer than 500,000 (three per cent) participated in strikes, and fewer still in the demonstrations' [176: 210]. Gareth Dale, however, maintains that from 16 to 21 June 'between 1 and 1.5 million people, six to nine per cent of the total population, participated in strikes, demonstrations and rallies' [35: 9]. Kowalczuk estimates that more than 700 different cities, towns, and villages were involved [116: 176]. Ostermann puts the figure at about 560 [166: 291]. If we are to believe GDR sources, 373 towns and villages were affected between 17 and 23 June, 'including 113 out of 181 district towns and 14 out of 15 regional capitals' [145: 44]. That the main centres of unrest were East Berlin, Halle, Dresden, Magdeburg, and Leipzig is not disputed [211: 129; 59: 184]. Some places remained relatively peaceful. For example, only a small minority of the Erfurt population actively demonstrated on 17 June: a mere seven factories went on strike and the security forces were generally effective at putting down disturbances [2: 56–7]. In the district of Karl-Marx-Stadt, the erstwhile and future Chemnitz, 'there were just a handful of strikes and no demonstrations' [200: 634].

Most of the demonstrators across the GDR in June 1953 were working class. By the end of the month, a total of 6,171 people had been arrested in connection with the unrest. As Pritchard has found, 'of the 5,296 individuals whose class origin is known, 65.2 per cent were workers' [176: 212]. Stibbe points out that 'the uprising found little support among East German students, intellectuals and church leaders' [145: 48]. Women, mainly housewives, probably constituted a minority of the demonstrators, certainly when it came to violent action; more research is required to clarify their role [200: 633]. According to Witkowski, the peasantry's persecution at the hands of the SED before the uprising 'kept many from risking punishment and thereby reduced the intensity of the protest in some villages' [225: 248]. Although historians such as McDougall [147: 26–67], Mitter and Wolle [152: 27–162], Bruce [22], and Witkowski [225] have established that members of the youth, bourgeoisie, and peasantry also participated, these elements were not typical of the social groups from which they came and were, in any case, far less numerous than the much larger working-class contingent [83a: 152]. Even so, they participated in significant enough numbers to render the 'workers' uprising' thesis inadequate.

Although some historians might take a different view, it is my contention that the fledgling GDR would have collapsed had it not been for the intervention of the Soviet army. There was, after all, very little time for the uprising to gain momentum, and if there had been a delay in the deployment of military force, the numbers of demonstrators would certainly have proliferated. As Pritchard has convincingly shown, 'mass working-class unrest did not subside with the crushing of the uprising, but continued into the late summer and early autumn of 1953' [134]. It was a similar picture in the countryside [225: 265]. For some weeks after 17 June, 'there were sporadic strikes, demonstrations, and isolated incidents across the GDR' [59: 185]. The USSR's Prime Minister, Georgi Malenkov, had himself conceded on 2 June 1953 that the East German regime was only kept in being by Soviet troops [127: 303]. Its vulnerability was further emphasized on 10 June when Soviet High Commissioner Vladimir Semyonov reportedly told Rudolf Herrnstadt, SED Politburo candidate member, that in 14 days' time the SED might not have a state anymore [93: 74]. Throughout the disturbances, sections of the party and People's Police were paralysed, some of their number even joining the demonstrators. This was certainly a revolution manqué, but not a revolution *per se*. Mitter and Wolle's term, 'revolutionary uprising' therefore lacks precision [152: 160].

In the light of all these factors, the events of 17 June 1953 are more accurately characterized as a popular uprising with revolutionary potential led by the workers. They were triggered by economic grievances, namely the regime's initial failure to rescind the ten per cent increase in work norms imposed on factory workers on 28 May. However, many demonstrations quickly became political. Bruce contends that political motives were already predominant at the beginning and warns us 'not to confuse the sparks which set off the uprising with the powder keg of fundamental political resistance' [22: 176]. But he overstates his argument. The fact that the uprising did not get under way fully until *after* the SED had caved in and revoked the increased work quotas late on 16 June does not necessarily prove his point. Many workers were unaware of the government's panicky decision and others who did sense the regime's weakness ended up doing little more than venting their anger against the Communists. Belatedly adopted slogans such as 'Free Elections!' and 'Down with the SED!' show that the demands of some demonstrators *became* political, often for economic and social reasons; they do not necessarily indicate that political motives were the primary cause of the disturbances in the first place [83a: 153]. That said, the proliferation of political demands does indicate revolutionary potential.

What did the strikers and demonstrators hope to achieve? East German society was deeply divided in 1953 and each of its various social groups had different objectives. According to Pritchard, their demands 'were often purely local and economic in character' [176: 211]. Even so, many workers did want to see the downfall of the government. One of their loudest chants was for the resignation of Ulbricht, who was as renowned for his goatee as Hitler was for his moustache; hence the slogan 'He with the beard must go!' and the burning of his portrait in public [94: 65]. Not only the SED General Secretary but also the country's President and Prime Minister were ridiculed: '*Spitzbart, Bauch und Brille sind nicht des Volkes Wille!*' ('Goatee – Ulbricht – Belly – the paunchy Pieck – and Spectacles – the glasses-wearing Grotewohl – are not the people's will!') [211: 124]. It is important to remember that, in the eyes of the workers, bringing down the SED-led government was not necessarily the same as overthrowing socialism. Some merely wanted to rid the system of its Soviet distortions. Having said that, demands for small and medium-sized factories to be re-privatized became increasingly overt after 9 June. Collective farms also began to dissolve themselves [152: 160]. According to Witkowski, peasants 'were not so much trying to overthrow the regime, something that many in June figured would happen anyway, but rather wanted to get revenge on local officials who had implemented policies and, perhaps more importantly, negate state power in their villages' [225: 264–5].

Unlike the situation in 1990, there was no consensus about what should replace the SED dictatorship. Although the overwhelming majority of East Germans bitterly resented Ulbricht's policies, this did not automatically make them advocates of Capitalist democracy, as some historians in the West have assumed [22; 152]. A mere eight years had passed since the end of the Second World War and it is naïve to believe that the population had metamorphosed into democrats [83a: 151]. For these same reasons, the thesis of GDR historians that the 17 June uprising was 'fascist' and 'counter-revolutionary' in character cannot be dismissed out of hand. After all, many Germans continued to harbour positive views of their former Führer [83a: 151] and nursed nostalgia for certain aspects of the Third Reich. Contrary to the claims of Cold War historians in the West, fascist sympathizers constituted a significant minority of the strikers and demonstrators on 17 June. Former Nazis had been sent down to work in the factories and were often involved in strikes. Swastikas did appear in certain places and Nazi songs were sung at a few demonstrations [176: 209]. If we take a 'counter-revolution' to mean a revolution opposing communism and reversing its results, then the events of 17 June 1953 could certainly have become one.

That said, there is no evidence to support SED assertions that this was an attempted putsch organized by the West – the so-called *Tag X* or 'D-Day' [7: 157–8]. If that had been the case, demonstrators would surely have targeted 'vital centres of communication such as railway stations, telephone exchanges and radio stations' [176: 209]. Pritchard notes that 'there was not one single instance anywhere in the GDR of protesters using firearms against the security forces' [176: 209]. The Western Powers did hope to 'roll back' communism by spreading capitalism and democracy to the Soviet bloc, but they were not interested in risking a Third World War. Instead of trying to undermine the GDR, the policy of the FRG in 1952 and 1953 was to stabilize it economically. In the view of many West Germans, the rising tide of refugees was threatening their fragile economic recovery. As for the administration of Konrad Adenauer in Bonn, it regarded the uprising with scepticism [200: 629]. While some Western agents may have encouraged the demonstrators (after all, the border between East and West Berlin was still open), they were not responsible for causing the unrest in the first place. On the contrary, it caught them entirely unawares. According to GDR sources, under five per cent of those brought in for questioning by the People's Police were inhabitants of West Berlin or the Bonn Republic [145: 45]. In contrast to the Hungarian revolutionaries three years later, the East German rebels of 1953 neither requested nor expected military assistance from Washington [200: 635].

When the uprising erupted, the only sentiment that the various social groups had in common was their hatred of Ulbricht and his policies. In the absence of Soviet armed intervention, this would have been enough to break the fragile 'Workers' and Peasants' State'. However, breaking a state is not the same as making one. Unlike the bloodless events of 36 years later, ultimate success might have been jeopardized by the disunity of the rebels. Although demands for German reunification were raised on 17 June 1953, they were not as deafening as in 1989–90. Instead of championing either the Federal Republic or the GDR, the demonstrators pinned their hopes on a new polity resulting from all-German free elections [200: 639]. The formation of such a state required the consent of all four occupying powers. Mitter and Wolle's speculation that German reunification was inevitable without the deployment of the Soviet military is therefore teleological [152: 160]. Dale has successfully rebutted those who interpret the 1989 Revolution as a consummation of 17 June 1953 [35: 189].

What were the consequences of the uprising? Ulbricht stayed in power by using the fall of Lavrenti Beria, the Soviet Minister of Internal Affairs, to discredit his opponents in the SED leadership. Among other things, Beria had been accused of proposing to sacrifice the GDR in favour of a 'bourgeois-democratic' Germany. Wilhelm Zaisser, the country's Minister for State Security, and Rudolf Herrnstadt, Chief Editor of the SED's daily newspaper *Neues Deutschland,* were purged from the Politburo and Central Committee in July 1953, before being expelled from the party in January 1954. Apart from enthusiastically endorsing the New Course and attacking the party's harsh administrative methods, they had tried to replace Ulbricht's personal dictatorship with a collective leadership. Zaisser was blamed for failing to unmask the 'counter-revolutionary conspiracy' before it struck. There is no evidence linking either of the two men with Beria, despite Ulbricht's allegations. Three other Ulbricht critics, Ackermann, Elli Schmidt, and Jendretzky, also lost their leadership positions. After the uprising, the Kremlin leaders became less keen on demoting the SED General Secretary, particularly since his removal from power had been a key demand of the demonstrators. But it took the Soviet rulers a few weeks to come round to this position. Henceforth Ulbricht would be known as First Secretary of the SED [84: 66–91].

A wave of repression then swept over the country. Within a month of the uprising, Justice Minister Max Fechner, a former Social Democrat, had been arrested for publicly defending the constitutional right to strike. He was replaced by the hard-line Hilde Benjamin. The number of people taken into police custody 'rose to between 8,000 and 10,000 by 1 July 1953 and to 13,000 by 1 August 1953' [145: 45]. Most of them were released without charge, but GDR courts imposed 1,524 prison sentences and the death penalty in two other cases [145: 45]. Moreover, several hundred anti-Communist 'suspects' were apprehended by Soviet authorities and banished to Siberia [145: 45]. As for the party, it was purged from top to bottom [84: 88]. The New Course was progressively watered down before being abandoned in June 1955 [84: 89].

Repression was only one side of the coin, however; welfare was the other. After 1953, according to Weitz, 'the state ensured that at least basic necessities were available to the population at reasonable prices. Food, housing, and utilities remained heavily subsidized and inexpensive until the very end of the regime' [222: 362]. To quote Stibbe: 'by September 1954 an estimated 3.7 billion East German marks had been redistributed to the general population' [145: 47]. In faux elections to the *Volkskammer* a month later, 99.46 per cent voted for the single lists [220: 296]. This result would have been harder to achieve without the party's integrated strategy of care on the one hand and coercion on the other. Welfare-totalitarianism was taking root in the GDR.

According to Ilko-Sascha Kowalczuk, Armin Mitter, and Stefan Wolle, one result of 17 June 1953 was the 'internal founding' of the GDR [115]. The term suggests that the fundamentals of East Germany were put in place only after the uprising. Yet the essential building blocks of the totalitarian state, such as the SED's monopoly on power, the command economy, the Stasi, and the Garrisoned People's Police, had already been laid before then. That said, it is true that the party and state apparatuses were reorganized after 17 June 1953. The Stasi was integrated into the Interior Ministry, before being made separate again in 1955. In 1952, the MfS employed more than 10,000 people, making it a larger organization than the Gestapo had been [200: 624]. Two years later, there were almost 14,900 agents on its books [134: 47]. By 1 November 1957, its apparatus had swollen to 17,400 staff [134: 54]. The 'Factory Combat Groups', which had begun to be established sporadically in various industrial areas in 1952, were developed quickly throughout the republic to become an essential pillar of national defence [134: 70–1]. Eventually numbering about 400,000 [59: 46], these co-called Combat Groups of the Working Class made their first public appearance at the annual May Day Parade in 1955 [220: 296]. As for the People's Police, they became progressively more militarized, while losing importance as an agency of the security bureaucracy [134: 71].

But it must be remembered that none of these things could have happened without the *external* guarantee afforded by the Soviet

Union. After 17 June 1953, the Kremlin accepted the unlikelihood of German reunification and began to shore up the 'Workers' and Peasants' State'. The GDR joined the Warsaw Pact, the Soviet bloc's equivalent to NATO, when it was founded in May 1955. This was in response to the FRG's admission to the Atlantic Alliance in the same month. It was not until the end of that year, however, that CPSU leaders adopted the policy of unconditional support for the GDR [184: 61–2]. Only then, on 18 January 1956, was East Germany permitted to establish a National People's Army (NVA) out of its Garrisoned People's Police.

In the light of these considerations, the somewhat different concept of a 'second founding' of the GDR has been suggested [91: 133]. This implies that East Germany actually imploded on 17 June 1953, which it did not. The Soviet occupation authorities had always exerted direct influence over the SED. It was only on 20 September 1955, more than two years *after* the uprising, that the 'full sovereignty' of the GDR was acknowledged and the office of Soviet High Commissioner abolished [220: 297]. Even then, East Germany's room for manoeuvre *vis-à-vis* the Kremlin remained restricted.

Neither can 17 June 1953 be depicted as the first stage in the downfall of the GDR [152: 27–162]. After all, the uprising helped to save Ulbricht's career. It did not even succeed in temporarily halting the construction of socialism, since that had already been decided at the beginning of June. The argument that the SED's leaders never trusted their population again after 17 June hardly amounts to much, given that they had never trusted it in the first place. In this respect, German playwright Bertolt Brecht's jibe that 'the people had forfeited the confidence of the government' was wide of the mark [215: 80]. As for the numbers of refugees fleeing the 'workers' and peasants' paradise', they peaked at 391,390 in 1953 [220: 295]. East Germany's best years still lay ahead. It would be more accurate to conceptualize the uprising as a successful rescue of the GDR.

Perhaps some of the reasons given for 17 June 1953 being a decisive watershed in GDR history [166: 415–21; 204: 78–95; 208: 69–104] have been overstated, particularly given the speed with which life returned to its previous routine. 'At least in the provinces', Allinson concludes, 'the legend which grew up around 17 June 1953 was far more substantial than the events of June 1953 themselves' [2: 56]. The uprising did not even finalize the divorce between the working class and the SED. According to Pritchard, 'in the weeks after the uprising, grievances, concerns and aspirations were often mutually shared by workers, SED members and functionaries alike' [134: 126]. In the long run, the failure of the uprising merely reinforced the pre-existing political apathy of most East Germans [2: 60, 62]. The regime's subsequent hard-line character was informed, not just by the traumatic memory of 17 June, but by the GDR's geopolitical position as a precarious state on the front line of the Cold War. It is telling that the revolutionaries of 1989 'made no reference to 1953' [200: 640]. Ultimately, the uprising became 'the turning-point' at which East German history 'failed to turn', to adapt G. M. Trevelyan's** arresting comment on the 1848 Revolutions in Europe [84: 79–80].

The impact of Khrushchev's attack on Stalin

At the 20th Congress of the CPSU in February 1956, the Soviet leader, Nikita Khrushchev, launched a sensational attack on the late Stalin, denouncing his 'cult of personality'. The 'secret speech' became public very quickly and sent shock waves through the Communist world. Both the Polish and the Hungarian governments crumbled, but that of the GDR remained intact. The extent to which East Germany's calm was deceptive is a moot point. Certainly there was some popular discontent, particularly in Magdeburg [59: 187–90; 147: 85–104]. Students at East Berlin's Humboldt University staged a rebellion, demanding an end to compulsory lessons in Russian language and Marxist–Leninist theory. A few intellectuals around Wolfgang Harich, Professor of Philosophy at the above university, and Walter Janka, head of the *Aufbau* publishing house, discussed the need for deStalinization. Harich even wrote a draft reform programme [84: 109–10, 145 n10]. But there was neither a rising nor a revolution.

How did the SED survive the aftershocks of Khrushchev's deStalinization campaign? The memory of 17 June 1953 was still raw in the minds of East Germans, serving as a powerful deterrent. In the intervening three years, the organs of state power had been strengthened. On 28 June 1956, there was an uprising in Poznań, Poland, caused primarily by inadequate wages and food supplies. According to Allinson, there was no attempt to emulate it because this would have implied that Germans were on the same level as the 'backward' Poles [2: 71]. That month saw price reductions in the GDR, covering 'textiles, bicycles, cameras, radios, and clocks' [220: 298]. The Soviet invasion of Hungary in early November 1956 chas tened those who harboured illusions about overthrowing communism. It also coincided with the Suez Crisis, an issue on which the population sympathized with the SED's position [2: 77]. GDR citizens were on the frontline of the Cold War. They dreaded the outbreak of hostilities between the Superpowers and any concomitant civil war with West Germany. This instilled a sense of caution.

On 16 November, 'all East German pensions were raised by 30 marks. The minimum pension was set at 105 marks' [220: 298]. Then, on 6 December, the GDR government announced the introduction of a 45-hour working week [220: 298]. A bonus system was also introduced [79: 500]. These attempts to improve the quality of life were not lost on the population, which was mainly concerned with material matters. In addition, they helped to prevent an alliance with the intellectuals, who were better off financially and more focused on ideological issues.

But the main reason for the relative quiet in East Germany was Ulbricht's refusal to liberalize. In his calculation, any attempt to do so would spark a reprise of 1953. When the students started demonstrating for political reform, he sent in the Combat Groups of the Working Class [84: 112]. Harich and Janka were put on show trial, receiving prison sentences of ten and five years, respectively (the former was amnestied in 1964, the latter gained early release in 1960 after international protest) [220: 266, 268]. On 4 March 1956, Ulbricht had flatly declared that Stalin was no longer a classic interpretator of Marxist theory [84: 115]. His own personality cult, however, continued unabated. Although a few erstwhile rivals, such as Merker and Dahlem, were partially rehabilitated, none were reinstated to their previous positions. SED leaders such as Karl Schirdewan and Fred Oelβner, who wanted to draw more far-reaching lessons from Khrushchev's 'secret speech', were purged in February 1958 [84: 114–44]. They had isolated themselves from both the intelligentsia and the wider population, fearing that any challenge to Ulbricht would imperil the system itself [79: 491]. The hard-line Erich Mielke replaced the more moderate Ernst Wollweber as Minister for State Security on 8 October 1957. According to Granville, 'the most influential factor in Ulbricht's survival was probably Soviet support' [79: 502]. The crucial factor is supposed to have been his success in averting a 'second Hungary' [152: 272]. Yet in January 1958, Khrushchev tried unsuccessfully to protect Schirdewan [84: 130–1]. Frank argues that the Soviet leader offered his hand to Ulbricht's opponents [50: 271]. If he did, their failure to take it ensured that deStalinization in the GDR remained a very limited affair.

The thesis advanced by Mitter and Wolle that 1956 marked the second stage in the downfall of the GDR lacks all foundation [152: 163–295]. Ulbricht went on the offensive in February 1957, declaring war on 'revisionism' and accelerating the tempo of Socialist development. In another victory for totalitarianism, the FDJ declared itself a Socialist youth organization in April of that year. The Protestant Churches were brought to heel and forced to accept the Socialist coming of age ceremony, the *Jugendweihe*, first introduced in 1954. Some studies have highlighted the often chaotic or incomplete fulfilment of SED objectives at grass-roots level [188]. Yet these findings are hardly surprising, given that the system was still under construction. Rather than casting doubt on the totalitarian nature of the regime, they actually show that East Germany was an inefficient totalitarian state.

The forced collectivization of agriculture in early 1960, known as the 'Socialist spring', consummated totalitarianism in the countryside. It also triggered a provisions crisis and a refugee surge. Nothing could more vividly demonstrate the ideological fanaticism and self-delusion of the SED leadership. Robert Havemann, East German chemist and national prize winner, later recalled the effect on the system's ability to produce reliable information:

Thus a member of Politburo, with whom I was travelling to India in the year of the great compulsory collectivization of agriculture in the GDR, believed that the difficulties the party was facing with collectivization in the countryside arose from the rural population having rushed into the process too enthusiastically, with the party struggling to restrain them in their headlong haste. This mind-boggling misinformation did, however, contain a grain of truth, albeit mutilated beyond recognition: the excessive zeal with which our worthy comrades in the countryside had pressurized the rural population into the Agricultural Co-operatives had led to a competition between districts and regions, with those party organizations naturally winning the laurels who were able to report whole villages at a time voluntarily joining. The party then subsequently excused the catastrophic decline in agricultural production in the first years of collectivization by reference to the excessive zeal of the rural population [229: 164].

With the formal completion of collectivization on 14 April 1960 [134: 146], the party announced that socialism had been built in the GDR.

On 10 February of that year, Ulbricht had been appointed Chairman of the newly formed National Defence Council. On 7 September, the country's President, Wilhelm Pieck, died. Five days later his largely ceremonial office was abolished and replaced by a Council of State. Ulbricht became its Chairman. He was now effectively Head of State as well as First Secretary of the SED. The East German dictator had never been so powerful.

Notes

* Alexis de Tocqueville, *The Old Regime and the Revolution* / translated by J. Bonner (NY, 1856), p. 214.
** G. M. Trevelyan, *British History in the Nineteenth Century (1782–1901)* (London, 1927), p. 292. Some years later, A. J. P. Taylor wrote that in 1848 'German history reached its turning-point and failed to turn'. See A. J. P. Taylor, *The Course of German History: A Survey of the Development of German History since 1815* (London, 1961 edn), p. 69.

3 Consolidation, 1961–71

Building the Berlin Wall

During the first 12 years of its existence, the GDR's greatest export was its people. By the time the Berlin Wall was built in 1961, 2.68 million citizens – most of them young workers and peasants – had fled the 'Workers' and Peasants' State'. Its population in 1949 was only 18.79 million, so that represented an average loss of more than 200,000 inhabitants per year [197: 214]. Since its borders with the FRG were closed in 1952, most absconded through the open border in Berlin, a bleeding wound in the East German body politic. They left for a variety of reasons, although 'material motives were undoubtedly paramount' [189: 30]. As Mark Landsman demonstrates, the Cold War was as much about consumption as ideological propaganda, spying, and the nuclear arms race. The SED was torn between its devotion to the Soviet model, which favoured heavy industry, and the need to keep pace with West German consumerism [118: 2, 13]. Apart from the pull of the increasingly magnetic Federal Republic, there were 'push' factors from within the GDR itself. The more repressive SED policies became, the greater the refugee outflow. Construction of the Berlin Wall, code-named 'Operation Rose', commenced on 13 August 1961. It was organized and overseen by Ulbricht's deputy, Erich Honecker. By 1970 there were '165 km of concrete slabs or metal fence, 3.5–4.2 m in height combined with ditches, anti-tank obstacles, watchtowers, floodlights, [and] dog kennels' [107: 58].

While the Wall was built primarily to stem the refugee flood, it would be a mistake to regard this as the only reason. As Maddrell has argued, it was also erected to protect the GDR from Western subversion, as the Communists claimed at the time [132: 829–47]. Agents were sent across the open border, not only to support resistance groups, but to encourage skilled workers to take up employment in the Federal Republic. The latter required their manpower to fuel its 'economic miracle'. Of course, this was the height of the Cold War and West Berlin was also infiltrated by Soviet and East German spies. Without the presence of American, British and French forces, the Capitalist island of West Berlin would eventually have been submerged in the Communist ocean.

That said, the Wall itself should not be seen as an act of aggression against the Western Powers, as claimed by some anti-Communists. After all, it was built on East German territory. The Chairman of the United States' Senate Foreign Relations Committee, Senator J. William Fulbright, even went so far as to state publicly on 30 July 1961 that he failed to comprehend why the GDR government had not exercised its 'right' to seal the border with West Berlin [211: 216]. When the SED began doing precisely what Fulbright recommended, US Secretary of State, Dean Rusk, proposed to the American President, John F. Kennedy, 'that the US government release a statement pointing out that the East German actions were aimed at their own residents and not at the Allies' [198: 161]. In reality, the Wall was only an act of aggression against those GDR citizens who wished to travel or emigrate to the West and against West Berliners who wanted to visit their friends and relatives in the GDR.

As Hope M. Harrison has demonstrated in a seminal study [88], Ulbricht pressured a reluctant Soviet leadership under Khrushchev into allowing him to build the Wall. Despite the exodus of refugees from East to West Berlin, the Soviets had consistently rejected pleas from the SED to seal off their side of the city. To do so, the Kremlin feared, would increase hostility to the Communists among Berliners and Germans on both sides of the Iron Curtain. It might also provoke the West into taking military action or imposing economic sanctions. Moreover, the technical difficulties involved in sealing the escape hatch were considered too great. Instead, Moscow attempted to persuade Ulbricht to adopt more moderate policies in the GDR. This, it was hoped, would convince East Germans of the virtues of socialism and stop them defecting to the West. Yet, as Harrison brilliantly demonstrates, Ulbricht successfully resisted these efforts [83b: 710]. Harrison's conclusion that 'to a large degree, the policies carried out in the GDR and in Berlin, the front line of the Cold War, were formulated by the East Germans, not the Soviets, and were often carried out against Soviet wishes' [88: 224] is particularly significant because the independent actions of Ulbricht in Berlin sometimes had the effect of undermining Khrushchev's credibility with the Western Powers. Furthermore, it disproves claims by indicted former East German leaders that the Soviets, not they, were responsible for the deaths at the Wall [83b: 711; 88: xiii–xiv, 212].

Harrison ascribes Ulbricht's ability to defy the Kremlin to a number of factors. Most important was his very strong personality, reflected in a determination to defend both his own interests and those of the GDR. Exercising what is best described as a tyranny of the weak over his Soviet masters, he turned his country's greatest weakness, the haemorrhaging of its skilled workforce, to his advantage by extracting maximum concessions from Moscow, usually in the form of economic aid. The more hard-line Ulbricht's policies became, the greater the outflow of refugees to the West. Paradoxically, the increasingly parlous state of the GDR enabled him to strengthen his bargaining position. It was Moscow's devotion to the 'first Workers and Peasants' State on German soil' that made Ulbricht's blackmailing of Khrushchev so effective. To further maximize his leverage over the Soviet leadership, Ulbricht played the two Communist giants, Khrushchev and Mao Zedong, off against each other. His manipulation of the worsening Sino-Soviet split to pressure Moscow into giving him more of what he wanted proved effective [83b: 711]. The East German dictator enjoyed another advantage over the Soviets in that he was much more focused on his country's internal problems than Khrushchev, who, as leader of one of the world's two Superpowers, had to devote his attention to a whole range of other matters. This was the perennial problem of an empire trying 'to project power from the centre to the periphery' [88: 226; 83b: 712].

On 15 June 1961, Ulbricht had declared at a press conference in East Berlin that 'no one has the intention of building a wall'. Yet, as Taylor points out, 'no one at the press conference had suggested that any such intention existed' [211: 203]. Khrushchev decided to grant Ulbricht's request to wall off East Berlin in early July. The decision was then confirmed at a Moscow meeting of the leaders of the Warsaw Pact states between 3 and 5 August [88: 192]. Once the concrete barrier was in place, it became more difficult for the East German 'tail' to 'wag' the Soviet 'dog' [83b: 712; 88: 7, 12, 229; 211: 166–93].

Did the Berlin Wall save the peace? East Germany's Communists certainly thought so [135: 155]. The argument even gained some currency in the West. On hearing of the Wall's construction, President Kennedy remarked that it was 'not a very nice solution but … a hell of a lot better than a war' [198: 161]. Having said that, the claim is a self-serving one as far as the SED is concerned. Its propagandists characterized the Wall as an 'anti-fascist protective rampart' designed to keep West German 'fascists' out rather than its own people in. The Bonn Republic was depicted as a safe haven for former Nazis bent on restoring the Capitalist, militarist and imperialist German past. In truth, fascism as an organized political force was dead in the FRG. Even if it had not been, the Western Allies would have kept the genie firmly in the bottle. The United States, Britain, France and West Germany had no intention of invading the GDR, although they did wish to undermine it. Neither were they willing to risk a war over East Berlin. The best evidence for this is their inaction while the Wall was being constructed. When notified of the events on 13 August, the British Premier, Harold Macmillan, commented that 'nobody is going to fight over Berlin' and refused to interrupt his golfing vacation in Scotland. President Kennedy carried on sailing [182: 719]. As for the Soviets, they were neither criminal nor foolhardy enough to invade the western part of the city. Khrushchev himself was terrified of provoking a war, which is why he instructed Ulbricht to proceed gradually, first using barbed wire to block access. The latter was to begin building a wall only if the Western Powers had not reacted after several days [182: 723, 725–26]. GDR troops who patrolled the border were carrying guns that were not loaded; only the Soviet forces behind them were armed [182: 725]. Given that the Western Powers knew none of this at the time, they were right to maintain a policy of non-intervention. The real danger lay in a military conflict breaking out by accident because of false perceptions on both sides and the volatile situation in the city. Even if this had happened, the two Superpowers would have done everything in their power to prevent a further escalation into a Third World War.

According to Harrison, 'Khrushchev came to see Ulbricht's concrete "Rose" not only as a way to save the GDR by stemming the refugee exodus, but also as a way to wall in Ulbricht in East Berlin so that he could not enact measures on the inter-Berlin border that would risk provoking an East-West military conflict' [88: 219]. However, it is worth noting that the construction of the Berlin Wall did not immediately end Communist attempts to breach Allied rights in Berlin, and in October 1961 an incident at Checkpoint Charlie threatened to turn the Cold War hot [182: 724]. In other words, the Wall actually increased Superpower tensions in the short run. It all began when an American diplomat by the name of Allan Lightner [211: 412] decided to attend the opera in East Berlin on 22 October 1961. Allied personnel were permitted to cross the borders unhindered. Yet his car was halted at the Wall by East German border guards, despite the fact that it carried US number plates. Lightner was denied entry unless he showed his passport but he refused: to have done so would have been equivalent to recognising the GDR and its authority over East Berlin. He asked in vain to see a Soviet officer [182: 724]. In the end, he was escorted across by US troops, although he never did make it to the opera that night [211: 405]. On 25 October, President Kennedy's personal representative in West Berlin, Lucius D. Clay, decided to test the Communists by ordering American tanks to take up positions along the Wall, facing the GDR. A variety of US vehicles drove to and fro across Checkpoint Charlie. Next day Soviet tanks approached the border. They lined up against those on the American side 'muzzle to muzzle' while Soviet MiG fighter jets flew overhead. All forces stationed in the city went on red alert. The smallest misunderstanding, for example an agitated private mistakenly firing his rifle, might have plunged Europe into armed conflict [182: 725]. That this brinkmanship did not go over the brink was at least partly down to good fortune. On 28 October, the Kremlin finally ordered the Soviet tanks to pull back. The Wall had not been breached, but the Allied right of access was upheld [182: 725].

In Taylor's view, 'Khrushchev had found himself forced by Ulbricht's aggressive anti-Western stance into going further than he wanted. Looked at this way, the decision to bring Soviet armour into East Berlin might be represented, not as an escalation, but as an attempt to claw back control of the crisis from the East Germans' [211: 420]. Whether or not this is true, many contemporaries in the West saw Khrushchev's actions as provocative. After the Cuban Missile Crisis of October 1962, the Checkpoint Charlie incident was probably the closest the Superpowers came to a direct military confrontation during the Cold War. As for the Wall, it remained the most dangerous border in world history, even if the situation in Berlin eventually became more stable and tensions abated.

Did the Berlin Wall save the GDR from oblivion? In the zero-sum game of the Cold War, its implosion would have seriously destabilized US–Soviet relations. However, the view that East Germany was on the brink of collapse does not bear close scrutiny. It could never have been dissolved as a political entity unless the Kremlin permitted it and there was absolutely no prospect of that happening in 1961. After all, the Soviet Union had hundreds of thousands of troops stationed on its territory, troops which it was prepared to use if necessary. As the westernmost outpost of the Soviet bloc and one of its two industrially advanced members (the other was Czechoslovakia), the GDR was regarded by Khrushchev as a 'superally' and a display window of socialism to the West [83b: 711; 88: 7].

As for the GDR's own security forces, they were being bolstered all the time. Neither were there any potentially destabilizing splits in the SED leadership. In other words, East German state power was strong. The efficiency with which Honecker executed Operation Rose is evidence enough of that. One must not confuse economic crisis with political collapse. Although the open border in Berlin cost the Republic billions – 'production losses alone were estimated at around 2.5 to 3 billion DM' [189: 25] – it was in Ulbricht's interests to exaggerate these losses so as to procure more aid from Moscow. Even without the Wall, economic growth in 1960 stood at 8.2 per cent [135: 46], hardly the 'recession' alleged by Taylor [211: 177]. This is not to deny the GDR's indebtedness or its 'serious shortages of raw materials and quality industrial products as well as food' [211: 176]. But the regime could have found other ways to lessen the outflow of its skilled workforce. It might have mitigated the 'push' factors by adopting more moderate policies, particularly with regard to the collectivization of agriculture (the People's Republic of Poland, after all, had managed to eschew collectivization). Emigrant labour could have been replaced by larger numbers of guest workers from other Communist countries. The government also had the option of introducing a more rigorous border regime by tightening controls at crossing points between East and West Berlin, although admittedly this would have been far less effective. Finally, increased financial assistance could have been provided by the Soviet bloc.

Why was there no large-scale resistance to the Berlin Wall? Fear of Communist repression was the most important factor. Ordinary East Germans remembered what had happened when Soviet tanks rolled on 17 June 1953 and did not want a repeat performance. The Stasi and People's Police were much stronger organizations than eight years previously. Furthermore, they were now augmented by the NVA and the Combat Groups of the Working Class. In a political clampdown between 13 August and 4 September 1961, more than 6,000 people were apprehended by the police [189: 34]. The judicial bureaucracy was also activated, causing a sharp rise in the number of prosecutions [135: 131]. Secondly, GDR citizens dreaded another war [59: 191–2], particularly as they had suffered so terribly in the last one. In the event of one breaking out, they would be expected to fight fellow-Germans on the front line.

Thirdly, there was widespread political apathy. Many Germans on both sides of the Iron Curtain felt helpless, since ultimately their fate was in the hands of the wartime Allies. From the perspective of a GDR province such as Erfurt, 'some 250 kilometres away from Berlin, the event was of less central importance' anyway [2: 119]. The secrecy with which Operation Rose was conceived and the suddenness of its execution took the whole country by surprise, making resistance seem pointless. Some Berliners even thought the border closure was temporary. After all, the sectoral checkpoints had been shut for short periods before [135: 120]. This gave rise to a 'wait-and-see attitude'. Fourthly, a minority of GDR inhabitants actually supported the Wall or at least saw some positive aspects to it. A few agreed with the decision for ideological reasons or were convinced by the regime's propaganda. The justification 'that the Berlin border problem had to be solved in the interests of the East German economy ... went some way towards diluting popular disapproval' [189: 35]. Some East Berliners had been angered by the fact that those living in the Western part of the city visited their capital to buy up subsidized produce in the shops. There was also resentment of the so-called border crossers who had earned more money than the typical GDR citizen by living in the East but working in West Berlin [189: 31, 35]. Fifthly, West German politicians did not encourage the GDR population to resist. Konrad Adenauer, Chancellor of the Bonn Republic, seemed detached and relatively unperturbed by events in Berlin. On that 'barbed wire Sunday' he failed to address the German people on television [182: 719].

When he finally visited the former Reich capital later that August he was booed [211: 399]. Willy Brandt, the Mayor of West Berlin, calmed the dangerously high emotions in his part of the city by leading peaceful and dignified protests [182: 721; 211: 323-4].

By sealing the border with West Berlin, the SED was able to establish greater control over its economy and population. The threat of emigrating had given those who stayed behind a degree of leverage over the authorities [187: 459]. According to Maddrell, the Wall also 'ended the most successful phase of espionage and subversion ever conducted by the Western states in Communist-held territory' [132: 843]. From this point on, ordinary GDR citizens had no alternative but to adjust to life in the 'Workers' and Peasants' Power'. Thus the totalitarian system became more efficient and East Germany started consolidating itself. Mitter and Wolle's argument that 13 August 1961 represented a stage in the downfall of the regime therefore lacks credibility [152: 297–366]. Equally problematic is Dietrich Staritz's claim that the day marked 'the secret foundation of the GDR' [204: 138]. Already at the start of the decade, the state's political organs were functioning smoothly. Reports of the country's imminent demise were greatly exaggerated. Continuity rather than change characterized many aspects of the dictatorship during the 1960s.

Even so, the Wall did not represent a clear victory for the SED. For a start, it could no longer blame all its problems on the Federal Republic. Despite the border closure, the economic crisis continued into 1962 [84: 160-1]. The falling population of the 1950s had guaranteed full employment, created job opportunities for women, eased the housing shortage, and facilitated social mobility. Another consequence of the open border had been that discontented citizens left the GDR rather than fomenting unrest. Now the party had to make concerted efforts to win them over [84: 160].

Of course, the Berlin Wall was a propaganda disaster for the SED because it advertised the fact that socialism could only be built behind barbed wire, concrete, and watch towers. From the outside at least, the GDR now looked like a prison or a concentration camp. Those who tried to escape were stigmatized as 'deserters from the Republic'. Estimates of the total number of fatalities at the Wall run between 86 and 227, depending on how the figures are calculated [211: 657–8]. One of the most iconic was that of 18-year-old Peter Fechter on 17 August 1962. His slow and agonizing death near Checkpoint Charlie in the centre of Berlin was caught on camera and scandalized the world [162: 133–5]. The Wall sliced through the heart and soul of the city, separating families, friends and loved-ones. People living on opposite sides of the same street now found themselves in different political universes, light years away from each other. The inhumanity of the 'anti-fascist protective rampart' did more damage to the GDR's reputation than anything else.

The limits of economic reform

Now that socialism had ostensibly been built, Ulbricht wanted it to work better. The building of the Berlin Wall, the continuing economic crisis and the beginnings of a reform discussion in the USSR created the prerequisites for a change in policy. Ulbricht realized that the economy required modernization if it was to keep pace with the 'scientific-technological revolution'. He deemed this to be essential if socialism was to demonstrate its superiority over capitalism. Improvements in living standards could be delivered only if productivity was raised. The New Economic System of Planning and Management (NES) was therefore launched in July 1963. It was the Eastern bloc's first economic reform programme. Centralized economic planning was to be somewhat reduced, factories granted a degree of independence, the market given greater consideration and incentives such as profits, bonuses and wage differentials introduced [84: 160-1]. Ulbricht also surrounded himself with a new breed of economic experts [129]. The extent of his metamorphosis from hard-line Stalinist to fanatical technocrat became clear only after the end of the Cold War [84; 106]. Without his initiative the NES would never have happened. In April 1967 it was rechristened the Economic System of Socialism (ESS) to underline its projected longevity. After that, central planners were instructed to concentrate on 'structure-determining' sectors of the economy like chemicals and electronic data processing, leaving more scope for autonomy in the 'non-structure-determining' areas [144: 123-4].

There is a debate among scholars as to the true meaning and significance of the NES/ESS. Some, such as Jörg Roesler, claim that it was a 'paradigm shift', a genuine attempt to marry plan and market [185]. Others, such as Arvid Nelson, argue that it was no such thing. According to the latter, the reforms were predicated on 'the absolute imperative of control. ... Liberalism and decentralization were window dressing' [158: 133–4]. The truth lies somewhere between these two positions. While the NES/ESS should not simply be dismissed as 'a more complicated iteration of the command economy' [158: 133], neither was it a consistent or thoroughgoing endeavour to combine plan and market. As McCauley pointed out, the aim was never to establish 'a Socialist market economy along Yugoslav lines' [144: 110]. The programme was also less radical than those adopted in Czechoslovakia and Hungary later in the decade [144: 110]. SED reformers believed fervently in the superiority of a planned economy; they just wanted it to function more efficiently. While some decentralization did take place, David Granick rightly warned against 'exaggerating the significance of the shift toward market coordination in East Germany under the New Economic System' [78: 164]. According to him, the country 'still leaned heavily ... upon direct coordinating orders from higher bodies to operating units' in 1970 [78: 164]. The number of people employed in the economic bureaucracy actually rose during the reforms [190: 91]. Contrary to the argument of Arnold Sywottek, the GDR economy remained totalitarian between 1963 and 1970 [210: 30].

Historians have largely judged the NES/ESS to be a failure [191: 174; 114: 41–72]. It would be more accurate to say that it failed to fulfil high expectations. Maier argued that the results were encouraging until 1970. The years 1968 to 1971 saw 'a spurt in annual growth rates to 5.2, 6.1, and 5.9 per cent, respectively' [133: 88]. Official Net Material Product (NMP) between 1960 and 1965 was 3.4 per cent; for the period 1965 to 1970 it was 5.2 per cent. While these figures might be biased upwards, Western estimates of the GDR's Gross Domestic Product (GDP) and Gross National Product (GNP) between 1960 and 1965 were 3 per cent and 3.5 per cent, respectively; for the period 1965 to 1970 they were 3.1 per cent and 5.1 per cent, respectively [133: 88]. Productivity also increased [179: 102] and East Germans experienced a 'general rise in living standards ... during the 1960s' [188: 189]. How much of this was due to the reforms is a moot point. After initial scepticism, the NES/ESS was broadly appreciated on the shop floor [188: 186, 188]. Overall, it 'led to significantly higher incomes for industrial workers as well as greater pressure to improve performance' [188:

186]. Despite numerous inconsistencies, according to Monika Kaiser, the NES/ESS 'achieved many of its goals' [98: 328].

That said, the reforms did not deliver the productivity gains needed for the GDR to catch up with, let alone overtake West Germany – one of Ulbricht's key objectives. Neither did they generate 'active political loyalty' to the regime among factory workers [188: 188]. For Nelson, the main problem was the lack of genuine market mechanisms. Instead, cybernetic theory was used 'to mimic the control, management, and economic feedbacks and flows of liberal capitalism to allocate resources more efficiently while retaining central control' [158: 262]. As Steiner points out, 'the reformers were trying to simulate market mechanisms without, however, introducing the foundations of a market economy. Neither the dominance of "people's ownership" nor the power of the party were questioned. Dogmatized Marxism as the theoretical basis was not abandoned. This contradiction marked the introduction and realization of the economic reform and inevitably resulted in inconsistencies' [208: 111]. According to Rubin, 'market mechanisms were introduced' but 'without any serious political will to relinquish ultimate authority over the economy'. This led to 'confusion and chaos'. In other words, 'rather than mixing the best of both systems, the reforms managed mostly to mix the worst of both systems' [191: 174]. But whatever the tensions in the NES/ESS, they were not severe enough to render it dysfunctional. Nelson's conclusion that the programme 'was doomed from the start' [158: 134] is therefore overly deterministic.

In the final analysis, the dilution and eventual abandonment of the reforms in 1970–71 owed more to politics than economics. The coming to power of Soviet leader, Leonid Brezhnev, in October 1964 strengthened the hand of the SED hardliners around Honecker. In a partial victory for them, the NES was scaled back somewhat in December 1965, although it was not jettisoned altogether, as Kettenacker claims [107: 58]. Earlier that month a key reformer and Chairman of the State Planning Commission, Erich Apel, committed suicide. He did so on the same day that the GDR signed a less than favourable agreement with the USSR, tying its trade more closely to the East [84: 164]. According to Kaiser, Soviet demands on East Germany 'undercut Ulbricht's plans to translate profits harvested in the course of reforms into benefits for workers' [98: 334]. The NES also represented a significant break with many past practices and enterprises needed time to adapt. Managers 'had to learn to think as entrepreneurs' and 'bank personnel had to acquire the skill to judge credit-worthiness' [144: 115]. The slowness of the reforms in showing the desired results further emboldened reform sceptics. Many party bureaucrats felt threatened by the NES/ESS and did everything in their power to subvert it [158: 134]. A report drafted for the Politburo averred that the reforms were being implemented slowly in agriculture because 'leading cadres do not understand the problems theoretically, shy away from their increased responsibility, manage in a routine manner and do not sufficiently involve the co-operative farmers in planning and management' [2: 134].

According to a critique of Ulbricht's economic policy written shortly after his downfall and signed by Honecker, the former SED First Secretary had wanted to go much further in reducing central planning, even proposing its replacement with a system of 'self-regulatory' mechanisms. Certainly Ulbricht is on record as endorsing the market as an important variable in the economic equation [84: 165]. Kaiser contends that he wished to move 'towards a "system of flexible prices" for industrial and economic goods as well as for service industries in 1969' [98: 328]. Ulbricht was also determined to preserve the remaining private and semi-state-owned businesses, which had proved so productive. He therefore insisted that the new constitution promulgated in 1968 include a clause granting them security of tenure [84: 166].

Despite his enthusiasm for the reforms, Ulbricht helped create the conditions for their abolition. In rather un-Marxist fashion, he pursued the primacy of politics over economics. As in the 1950s, economic growth targets were set too high in order to achieve the fanciful aim of 'overtaking' West Germany [84: 168]. Ulbricht's obsession with forcing the pace of the 'scientific-technological revolution' led him to overemphasize 'structure-determining' areas of the economy at the expense of the consumer industries. Shortages of essential goods appeared in the shops [157: 35]. The situation was worsened by the harsh winters of 1968–9 and 1969–70. On 8 September 1970, while Ulbricht was on vacation, Honecker seized the initiative. A Politburo resolution was passed correcting imbalances in the economy and significantly strengthening the powers of the central planning agencies. Ulbricht could only look on as the

ESS was effectively scrapped at the SED's 14th Central Committee Plenum in December [84: 169].

Historians have debated whether the reforms represented a 'missed opportunity' for the GDR. To argue, as Roesler does, that they could have prevented the country's economic decline in the 1970s and 1980s is to deny the systemic problem of state control [186]. As Ross has concluded, the reforms 'represented an attempt to slow the rate of rotation of the downward spiral, not to tackle the underlying problems' [190: 94].

The impact of events in Czechoslovakia

The political climate had been frozen by the Warsaw Pact's invasion of Czechoslovakia on 20–21 August 1968. In order to achieve 'socialism with a human face', Alexander Dubček's reform-Communist government had introduced a programme of economic and political liberalization. When Soviet tanks arrived to reverse it, the eight-month Prague Spring turned into a 21-year Russian winter. The effect was to freeze experimentation and innovation across the Eastern bloc. Although the icy winds were not felt immediately, Ulbricht's economic reforms looked increasingly out of place in the emerging era of conservatism – a fact that was not lost on Honecker and his allies.

According to Wolle, the overwhelming majority of East Germans seemed indifferent to the rape of Czechoslovakia. In his view, this was due to the sheer power of the invading armies, deep scepticism regarding the reformability of socialism, and 'widespread deference towards authority' [227: 182–3]. Allinson cautions against the assumption 'that the GDR was gripped with enthusiasm for Dubček's liberal socialism'. Apparently, some East Germans looked down on their Czechoslovak neighbours, believing their problems were the result of 'economic backwardness' [2: 148]. None of this contradicts Fulbrook's argument that 'the extent of popular unrest and of splutterings of revolt was far greater than ever previously imagined' [59: 194]. But SED control was strong and protest remained atomized.

In 1993 Mitter and Wolle described the crushing of the Prague Spring as a 'stage' in the downfall of East Germany [152: 367–482]. Even if the subsequent stagnation undermined the long-term prospects of the Soviet bloc, East Germany did not plunge into decline as a result of these events. On the contrary, its trajectory improved somewhat in the early 1970s. By preventing the country's infection by the virus from Prague, the Warsaw Pact invasion actually enhanced its stability. As a Cold War state with little popular support, the 'Workers' and Peasants' Power' was incapable of sustaining emancipation.

Neither does Hartmut Zwahr's claim that in 1968 the dream of a Socialist society 'shattered in the heads of the people' bear close scrutiny [72: 161]. For most East Germans that dream had never existed in the first place. For others it was a nightmare. Surely any illusions they might have harboured about the Communist system had been dispelled during the crises of 1953, 1956, and 1961. Those who yearned for 'socialism with a human face' were given fresh hope by Soviet leader, Mikhail Gorbachev, in the late 1980s. Having said that, 'the Czechoslovak crisis finally established the bankruptcy of the GDR's own media in the public's perception and confirmed the long-standing trend towards reliance on western broadcasts' [2: 154].

Ulbricht had been one of the fiercest advocates of military intervention. At the time, his government gave the impression that GDR troops participated directly in what was the largest military operation in Europe since the end of the Second World War. After 1989 it emerged that NVA involvement was only indirect. Perhaps the Warsaw Pact leadership wanted to avoid aggravating the situation by sending German troops into Czechoslovakia 30 years after Hitler's annexation of the Sudetenland [227: 153–4].

Totalitarianism and welfare

Ulbricht's changes to the East German polity during the 1960s did little more than refine its totalitarian characteristics. To reflect the fact that socialism had been built, the SED's guaranteed majority in parliament was increased. This was done mainly by boosting the number of deputies from the mass organizations, most of whom were Communists [144: 118]. In July 1965 a new electoral law was approved enabling voters to select candidates on the single list they preferred. Those failing to poll 50 per cent would not be elected. However, hardly anyone dared make use of this opportunity because 'most of the voting was open, not secret' [144: 121].

When national elections were held on 2 July 1967, 99.93 per cent still endorsed the single list [220: 311].

Pseudo-democracy was bolstered as the SED sanctioned 'permanent production councils, production committees ... more commissions of representative institutions at local level and greater responsibilities for mass organizations' [144: 126]. According to the party, the 'scientific-technological revolution' necessitated increased contact between employees and managers [144: 126]. A plebiscite was held on 6 April 1968 to ratify the country's second constitution, which came into force three days later. Apparently 94.49 per cent voted 'yes' [220: 312], slightly less than the usual near-unanimous endorsement of the government at general elections. Even so, this was anything but a free vote. Following a public 'consultation' before the plebiscite, clauses protecting freedom of conscience and worship had been added to the draft constitution, as had a passage granting Members of Parliament immunity from prosecution [220: 113]. But given that the political rights enshrined in GDR law were little more than window dressing anyway, the first two clauses were largely nominal. The immunity clause could even be used to protect corrupt deputies who had not been democratically elected in the first place.

In 1963 the regime had instigated a cultural thaw and announced a more relaxed policy towards the country's youth. Both policies came to an abrupt end in December 1965 [1; 147: 153–201; 134: 171–89]. By introducing conscription on 24 January 1962, the SED created a perfect opportunity to extend its ideological influence over young males [144: 116–17]. Throughout the decade as a whole, the tentacles of the Stasi continued to grow, even if the octopus itself became less violent. According to Bruce, there were '100,000 informers in Ulbricht's East Germany, a higher number per capita than anywhere else in Eastern Europe' [21: 808]. By the time Ulbricht was deposed in 1971, the number of full-time MfS staff had grown to 45,580 – a rise of more than 300 per cent on 1952 [21: 808].

On the other hand, there were advances in the social sphere. A five-day working week, every fortnight, was rolled out in 1966 and the following year it was extended to every week. Then the basic holiday entitlement was raised by three days to 15 working days [144: 116]. Pensions were also increased [144: 181, 239]. A new 'Law on the Unified Socialist Educational System', guaranteeing 'all citizens an equal right to education', was passed on 25 February 1965 [144: 120]. Bound up with this right was the SED's desire for ideological control.

The fall of Ulbricht

According to accounts written during the Cold War, it was partly Ulbricht's opposition to *détente* and *Ostpolitik* (the FRG's policy of rapprochement towards Soviet bloc countries initiated by the Social Democrat Chancellor Willy Brandt in 1969) that led to his replacement as SED First Secretary on 3 May 1971 [27: 80–3; 199: 165; 142: 100–1, 115]. His successor, Erich Honecker, was supposed to be more amenable. This conventional wisdom survived the collapse of East Germany and the opening of its archives [67: 138; 179: 104–5; 198: 252; 140: 73; 143: 79]. Then, in the late 1990s, new scholarship emerged which demonstrated that it was Ulbricht's determination to pursue rapprochement with Bonn without first consulting Moscow that contributed to his overthrow. Honecker adopted a much more sceptical position [106: 324–69; 84: 170–83; 50: 401–9]. According to this interpretation, Ulbricht wanted better relations with the FRG's fledgling Social Democrat–Liberal coalition in order to benefit the GDR's economy. If he could gain access to Western markets, technology and expertise, the GDR could become more appealing, increasing the prospects of German reunification under Communist auspices [47: 184]. In his closing speech to the 14th SED Central Committee Plenum in December 1970, Ulbricht violated party policy by alluding to the virtues of an all-German confederation [84: 181]. Certainly there are indications that he was considering some kind of economic confederation with the Federal Republic [209: 529]. On the issue of Berlin, however, he would brook no compromise [84: 182–3; 142: 111–15].

In the view of M.E. Sarotte, 'Instead of asking which of the two men was more pro- or anti-*Ostpolitik*, it is more informative to look at the extent to which they were willing to follow Moscow's lead at all times, including sudden changes of course' [193: 110]. For her, 'perhaps the most convincing evidence that the "pro- or anti-*Ostpolitik*" question is irrelevant is the fact that, after assuming office, Honecker allowed the German–German talks simply to continue as before. ... the crucial criterion that had brought

Honecker into power had not been his anti-*Ostpolitik* stance but rather his willingness to conform to Soviet desires' [193: 110–11]. Yet, according to Smyser, Honecker probably 'played the most important role' in engineering or at least permitting Brandt's downfall on 6 May 1974. He did this by refusing to recall the East German spy, Günter Guillaume, from the Bonn Chancellery. With the unmasking of Guillaume, Brandt had to resign. Brezhnev was furious [198: 268–9]. The GDR's spymaster, Markus Wolf, later wrote that the Stasi's role in ending the Chancellorship of Brandt 'was equivalent to kicking a football into our own goal' [226: 189]. But it enabled Honecker to 'better control the pace and direction of inner-German *détente*' [198: 269].

That said, Ulbricht had been more proactive in defending what he perceived to be his country's national interests. For example, he seems to have been the driving force behind the Erfurt and Kassel talks between Brandt and Willi Stoph held in March and May 1970 respectively (Stoph had succeeded Grotewohl as the GDR's Prime Minister in 1964) [143: 89]. One participant later recalled that, as preparations for the encounters got underway, 'Soviet officials made nervous enquiries at the SED Central Committee in their efforts to keep abreast of the East German initiative' [143: 89].

During the period of consolidation, Ulbricht took an increasingly independent stance on a range of issues from economic reform to policy towards China [84: 176, 215]. He even took to describing the GDR as a Socialist model to be followed by other nations [84: 168, 186], thereby implicitly challenging Soviet hegemony within the Eastern bloc. His insubordinate behaviour went down particularly badly in the Kremlin after the crushing of the Prague Spring. On 28 July 1970, Brezhnev warned Honecker: 'We held on to the CSSR ... it will also not be possible for him to rule without regard to us ... After all, we have troops in your country' [177: 280–1]. The following month, on the second anniversary of the Warsaw Pact invasion of Czechoslovakia, Ulbricht told a meeting of the CPSU and SED leaderships in Moscow: 'In the cooperation we want to develop ourselves as a genuine German state. We are not Belorussia, we are not a Soviet Republic. So, genuine cooperation' [202: 697]. The day before, on the 20 August, Brezhnev had met with the SED leadership without Ulbricht. He impressed on them the importance of the GDR having a structure 'like the Soviet Union and other Socialist countries' [178: 341]. On 31 March 1971,

Ulbricht addressed the 24th Congress of the CPSU. He pointedly reminded his audience that he had met Lenin personally in 1922. Lenin, he lectured his hosts, had advised Russian comrades to learn from their German counterparts. This would be his last independent speech [122: 156; 84: 186]. Shortly after the Congress finished, 'Soviet press releases upgraded Honecker's status' [198: 253].

The Ulbricht era was brought to an end by the Soviet and GDR leaderships; the East German population played no role whatsoever. Kaiser's conclusion that Ulbricht's resignation was 'in the end voluntary' [106: 438] is rather unconvincing. The SED leader himself 'admitted that he had found it difficult to step down' [144: 150]. On 21 January 1971, 13 of the 21 members of the SED Politburo had signed a secret letter to Brezhnev asking for his support in securing the First Secretary's resignation. Ulbricht was accused of pursuing his own policies regardless of collective decisions [177: 297–303]. Back in East Germany after the 24th CPSU Congress, Honecker 'visited Ulbricht at the latter's retreat in Dölln, accompanied by a detachment of the private guard force for senior GDR officials. Brandishing machine pistols, the guards surrounded Ulbricht's compound and blocked all entrances and exits. When the guards had taken their posts, Honecker went in and, after a conversation of an hour and a half, gained Ulbricht's agreement to leave office' [198: 253]. After being practically forced to resign, Ulbricht remained in the Politburo and continued to serve as Chairman of the State Council. To ensure his cooperation, he was also appointed to the specially created but meaningless position of Honorary Chairman of the SED. The powers of the Council of State were reduced and he was increasingly ostracized. On 24 June he was stripped of his functions as Chairman of the National Defence Council. His relations with the new Honecker leadership went from bad to worse [84: 187–93]. Ulbricht even became a victim of the surveillance system he had done so much to create [209: 505]. After his death on 1 August 1973, the former dictator became an 'unperson' [84: 193].

4 Conservatism, 1971–7

Foreign policy

When Honecker came to power in 1971 East Germany reverted to
being Moscow's most dependable ally. This is reflected in the constitutions of 1968 and 1974. While Ulbricht did no more than assert
'all-round co-operation and friendship' with the USSR, Honecker
declared the GDR 'forever and irrevocably allied' with the Soviet
Union [84: 183]. During the 1970s, the 'Workers' and Peasants'
Power' achieved full international recognition, joining the United
Nations as its '133rd member' on 18 September 1973 [220: 319].
The two Germany's recognized each other on 21 December 1972
when they signed the Basic Treaty. Before that month, the GDR
enjoyed formal diplomatic relations with only 38 countries. By
1978, the number had risen to 123 [221: 432–3]. To quote Jonathan
Steele, this was 'the state that came in from the cold' [207].

The FRG continued to pursue *Ostpolitik* in some form or another
until the GDR's collapse 20 years later. A debate then ensued over
whether it did more to stabilize or destabilize the SED dictatorship. Its original aim was '*Wandel durch Annäherung*' or 'change
though rapprochement', to quote Brandt's aide Egon Bahr in 1963
[69: 66]. This came to mean gradually liberalizing the Communist
system by penetrating it economically, politically and culturally.
Increased contact between East and West Germans was supposed
to reduce Cold War tensions, make the Iron Curtain more perme-
able and facilitate German reunification in the long run. On the
one hand, *Ostpolitik* strengthened the GDR by providing desperately
sought-after international recognition and financial assistance.
On the other, it helped dissolve 'the ideological cement' that held
the system together [213: 20]. Brandt's peace policy went down well
with most East Germans, as evidenced by the ecstatic welcome he

received in Erfurt [193: 42–54]. It thereby discredited SED propaganda about West German imperialism. The new opportunities for contact between East and West Germans served to highlight the widening gap between the two republics [179: 106]. By improving relations between the FRG and the Soviet Union, *Ostpolitik* created an essential prerequisite for German reunification.

East Germany's Foreign Minister, Otto Winzer, reportedly responded to Bahr by describing *Ostpolitik* as 'aggression in felt slippers' [69: 204]. In the 1970s, the SED reluctantly accepted the policy, still fearful of the potential threat to its domestic authority [142]. To protect the country against Capitalist subversion, the party intensified its policy of *'Abgrenzung'* or 'delimitation' from West Germany. This meant pointing up ideological, political, socio-economic and cultural differences with the Federal Republic. Measures were taken to increase indoctrination about the dangers of the 'class enemy' in schools and workplaces [143: 101]. Military propaganda was also stepped up [37: 185]. GDR institutions were renamed to disassociate them from any notion of a shared German culture. A new category of citizens was invented – the 'so-called *Geheimnisträger* (or "secret-carriers") ... who by virtue of their supposedly sensitive positions were forbidden to have any interactions with Westerners' [143: 101–2]. In the revised constitution of 1974, the GDR was no longer defined as 'a Socialist state of the German nation' but as 'a Socialist state of workers and farmers'. The clause pledging the 'gradual rapprochement of the two German states until their unification on the basis of democracy and socialism' was deleted altogether [84: 182]. Honecker even banned the words of the GDR national anthem because they referred to 'Germany, united Fatherland' [26: 113].

Ostpolitik went hand in hand with *détente* during the 1970s. Both facilitated a partial thaw in the Cold War. At the 1975 Conference on Security and Cooperation in Europe, Honecker together with the other Soviet bloc leaders, signed the Helsinki Agreement. 'Basket Three' guaranteed their citizens basic human rights. In return for these concessions, the Western Allies formally accepted the reality of Soviet hegemony in Eastern Europe since the end of the Second World War. Honecker had no intention of properly implementing the accord, particularly as it was not binding in international law. But when the full text appeared in *Neues Deutschland*, the SED daily sold out for the first time in its history. The human rights stipulations contained therein gave a considerable morale boost to ordinary East German citizens, who now set about using them to hold their Communist rulers to account [145: 161–2]. As Pulzer points out, 'Helsinki monitoring committees became a focus of dissent as time went on' [179: 107]. For obvious reasons, East Germans were particularly interested in the right to visit friends and relatives in the Federal Republic. Within 12 months of the agreement, more than 100,000 people had applied for permission to leave the GDR [33: 358]. Soon the East German government was being pilloried at home and abroad for violating the very human rights provisions it had solemnly signed up to. This discredited the state in the eyes of its population and the international community [145: 162].

The Stasi had to refine its methods during this decade, so as not to jeopardize the GDR's newfound international respectability. Thus the most obvious human rights abuses were mitigated. 'Operational decomposition' or '*Operative Zersetzung*' now became the key component in a system of 'silent repression', as Hubertus Knabe characterizes it [40: 112]. This involved 'decomposing' so-called hostile-negative groups by deploying a vast arsenal of 'dirty tricks' against them. Examples included the spreading of false rumours, bugging of telephones, interference with post, and burglary [40: 112–13].

That said, *détente* and *Ostpolitik* failed to liberalize the GDR. Their Trojan horse aspects led to a rapid growth in the size of the Stasi after 1971. Within two years of the Helsinki Agreement, it had augmented its staff by over 10,000 [112: 142]. Honecker was already obsessed with state security because he had served as Central Committee Secretary for Cadres and Security under Ulbricht. In 1971, he brought the head of the secret police, Erich Mielke, into the Politburo as a candidate member. Mielke went on to become a full member in 1976 [220: 273]. This reflected the increasing importance of the MfS in Honecker's East Germany. During the 1970s the Stasi hypertrophied by an astonishing 60 per cent, from 50,000 to almost 80,000 official employees [195: 11]. As Childs observes, 'one noticeable trend in the Honecker period was the growing numbers of military, police and state security members' of the Central Committee [26: 12].

Two unintended consequences of *détente* and *Ostpolitik* were therefore the expansion of the secret police and a sharpening of the SED's ideological offensive. In these respects the GDR became more totalitarian during the 1970s. In 1974, Honecker had declared that there was 'no alternative to the growing role of our party in the life of society' [220: 132]. The original aim of *Ostpolitik* was to bring about small improvements in the daily lives of East and West Germans. Yet according to Sarotte, 'for the bulk of the *détente* era, the wishes of the GDR's average citizens are mostly notable for their absence' [193: 53]. Her verdict is largely true in the realm of politics but less so in the field of socio-economic policy.

Socio-economic policy

How should we define conservative totalitarianism? Essentially, it amounted to more mollification and less mobilization of the population. After 1971, the SED abandoned Ulbricht's utopian goals for the future and instead turned its attention to improving the present in what became known as 'really-existing socialism' – a term coined in 1973 [144: 150]. After the Eighth Party Congress in June 1971, the raising of living standards through consumerism and welfare became the order of the day. This was supposed to boost the economy by spurring labour productivity. If workers lived better, so the theory went, they would be grateful and work harder. The policy became known as 'the unity of economic and social policy'. It amounted to a social contract between the SED and the wider population: comply with the party's demands and it will reward you. This was a softer form of control suited to the new age of *détente* and *Ostpolitik*. Furthermore, as Madarász points out, Honecker 'reacted directly to the economic crisis … which had resulted in public demands for an improvement in living standards' [130: 31]. The fall of the Polish government in 1970 had shown the dangers of ignoring the popular mood on this issue. Thus the policy was a compromise on Honecker's part [130: 167], although it was one he was happy to make. After all, it fitted with his idea of socialism forged during the Great Depression of the 1930s, according to which everybody was guaranteed protection against poverty [114: 80–1].

As the economy was recentralized following the jettisoning of the ESS, it became more totalitarian. Most of the remaining private and semi-private enterprises in the GDR were nationalized in 1972. The motives for this policy were political, not economic

[114: 78]. They 'had more to do with Honecker's drive for insti-
tutional standardization than anything else' [114: 79]. There can
be no doubt that Honecker and Brezhnev were in full agreement
on the issue [114: 79]. When the former took over as SED First
Secretary, these private and semi-state-owned businesses still
employed 470,000 workers and comprised 11.3 per cent of production in East Germany. GDR efficiency specialist Harry Meier even
called them 'the "secret weapon" of the economy' [114: 77]. Now
they were condemned as 'Capitalist remnants'. The nationalizations delivered what one historian has called a 'knockout' blow
to middle-class entrepreneurs [105]. That the bourgeois parties
collaborated fully demonstrates how faithfully they were fulfill-
ing their roles as 'transmission belts' within the totalitarian system. According to Kopstein, the nationalizations 'contributed in
no small way to the economic decay of the GDR in the 1970s and
1980s' [114: 80]. What East Germans called 'the thousand little
things' disappeared from the shops [94: 168–71]. This undermined
the very 'consumer socialism' Honecker was trying to promote. As
Childs concludes, the policy was 'a self-inflicted injury' [26: 25].

In the wake of the Eighth SED Congress a range of new social
policies were introduced. Women were among the chief beneficiaries. Abortion became legal in 1972 [89] and contraceptives were
provided free of charge. To counteract the falling birth rate, a pro-
natalist policy was adopted. This proved successful. Maternity leave
was extended from 18 to 26 weeks and mothers were given 1,000
marks for every newborn infant. Mothers were allowed to take 12
months unpaid leave without losing their jobs or social benefits.
Following the birth of a second baby the mother was permitted
12 month's leave on sick pay. Mums in full employment with three
children were only required to work 40 hours a week (extended to
include mothers with two offspring in 1977) and entitled to three
weeks holiday instead of 18 days without any cut in wages. Working
mothers with kids under the age of six were exempted from shift
work or overtime. Women in full-time jobs were granted a day off
each month for domestic chores, if they had children under 18
years old. Females over the age of 40 and single dads were also
given a day off each month [144: 180]. Moreover, crèche and nursery school facilities were expanded. This opened up new opportunities for women to go out to work. While no more than 25.6 per
cent of infants up to the age of three were cared for in crèches in

1970, this had already climbed to 40.3 per cent in 1974 and would reach 60 per cent by the end of the decade. The percentage of children in nursery schools rose from 59.7 in 1970 to 76.3 four years later [144: 182].

Pensions went up in 1971 and once more a year later when they increased by 20 per cent [144: 181]. The SED also cut the number of compulsory hours in the working week and reduced flat rents below the already insubstantial one mark per square metre [114: 81]. Furthermore, it undertook the heavy subsidization of prices for a wide variety of staple commodities, such as food and children's garments [114: 81]. Charges for energy and local public transport were 'frozen' as well [94: 167]. Honecker's flagship policy was a housing programme launched in 1976 [114: 81]. It aimed 'to build three million flats by 1990 and thereby solve the "housing question as a social problem"' [94: 167]. Already between 1971 and 1975, 400,000 new homes had been constructed and some 290,000 refurbished. In the second half of the decade, progress would be even more impressive with this area of the economy being one of the few 'to overfulfil its plan' [144: 179].

These improvements in welfare [204: 203–5, 221–2] show that socialism did have a human face, at least in the field of social policy. It would be simplistic to argue that they were nothing more than a massive bribe to tighten ideological control over a restive population. The SED also regarded them as a way of raising living standards, creating a fairer, more equal society and securing international recognition. Millions of East Germans benefitted. That said, one can hardly deny that they helped to buttress the totalitarian system. In this sense, the regime was Janus-faced. After its Ninth Congress in May 1976, the party responded to popular demand by promising improvements in working and living conditions over the next four years [144: 166, 254]. Various concessions were granted. It was decided to increase retirement pensions on 1 December and to raise the minimum wage from 1 October [144: 166]. A Council of Ministers' decree of 14 October, which took effect in January 1977, boosted the holiday entitlement for shift workers and working mums with seriously disabled offspring [144: 254]. Three days later, on 17 October 1976, pseudo-democratic elections to the *Volkskammer* and *Bezirk* assemblies were staged. These resulted in a 99.86 per cent endorsement of the single lists [220: 323]. No doubt the electorate's participation was facilitated by the social gains achieved that year. Since the voting age had been lowered from 21 to 18 in June [144: 254], a larger percentage of the population took part in the charade.

Honecker had every reason to be satisfied. At the Ninth Party Congress, where he was renamed General Secretary of the SED, he had declared East Germany's 'dictatorship of the proletariat' to be 'the highest form of democracy' [220: 150]. Needless to say, this was an ideological self-delusion. Less than a fortnight after the parliamentary elections, he also became Chairman of the State Council [220: 324]. Now that he was head of party and state, his power looked unassailable. A new party programme of 1976 issued GDR citizens with guidelines for a 'Socialist way of life', regulating 'private life' and 'social relations'. The SED had reaffirmed its totalitarian mission [196: 227].

Cultural policy

At the Eighth Party Congress, Honecker admitted that artistic composition in East Germany displayed symptoms of 'superficiality, formality and boredom' [27: 218]. In December 1971, at the SED's Fourth Central Committee Plenum, he proclaimed: 'If one proceeds from the social premise of socialism, there can be in my view no taboos in the realm of art and literature. This applies both to questions of content and style – in short, to the concept of artistic mastery' [39: 144]. Thus began a five-year thaw in the field of culture, which went beyond art and literature. A permissive attitude was also adopted towards jeans, miniskirts, long hair, and beat music. In May 1973, Honecker announced that all GDR citizens were permitted to switch on Western radio and television, something many of them were doing already [39: 145].

According to Madarász, the 'no taboos' period amounted to 'an important compromise in cultural policy' [130: 174]. If so, it was granted from a position of strength, not weakness. It was also one which the regime had no difficulty rescinding. By allowing artists and writers the chance to explore new themes, Honecker hoped to make them feel more beholden to the party. His continued insistence that artists and writers work within the ideological framework of socialism placed strict limits on liberalization. This was a more subtle means of exercising control, designed to bolster

East Germany's image in the era of *détente* and *Ostpolitik*. Since the cultural intelligentsia was heavily penetrated by the Stasi and most of its members subscribed to some kind of socialism anyway, Honecker must have felt assured of success [39: 145–6]. Even so, the ensuing effervescence of criticism and experimentation went too far for the SED's liking. Inadvertently, the policy brought 'cultural subversives' out into the open so that they could be dealt with more effectively.

The 'no taboos' policy had been languishing for some time before it came to a definitive end on 16 November 1976. On that day, the balladeer and poet, Wolf Biermann, was stripped of his GDR citizenship and forbidden from re-entering the country while on a concert tour of West Germany. In the words of *Neues Deutschland*, it was for 'gross violation of his civic duties and a hostile public performance against our Socialist state' [27: 223]. The regime had planned the expatriation in detail some three years earlier [130: 44]. Biermann might have been a Communist but he was also a dissident and this put him beyond the pale in the eyes of the SED leaders.

Twelve leading intellectuals sent Honecker an open letter of protest the following day. About 100 others then signed their names. This was an unprecedented event in the country's history. FRG newspapers reported 'that in factories in Berlin and Jena there were demonstrations of solidarity with Biermann' [27: 223]. The SED's response was to launch a campaign of persecution against the signatories which included bans, imprisonment, ejection from the Writers' Union, and expulsion from the GDR [144: 186]. Had it not been for widespread protests in the West, the punishments would probably have been even harsher [27: 224]. On 26 November 1976, one of the country's most distinguished academic dissidents, Professor Robert Havemann, was placed under house arrest. On 23 August 1977 Rudolf Bahro was apprehended for publishing his critique of really-existing socialism, *The Alternative*, in West Germany [220: 324]. Both Havemann and Bahro were convinced Communists who sought merely to reform the system.

David Clay Large rightly avers that the 'expulsion of dissident intellectuals, like the sale of political prisoners to Bonn, proved to be an effective way to retard the development of a strong political opposition' [119: 514]. In other ways, however, the Biermann Affair amounted to a spectacular own goal on the part of the regime.

By exposing the dictatorship as intolerant, insecure and repressive, it sullied the international reputation of the 'Workers' and Peasants' Power'. At home, it permanently soured relations between the party and the intelligentsia. The SED's punishment of critical but generally sympathetic cultural figures undermined its own support base. As McCauley observes, 'until 1976 there had been a net inflow of writers and artists into the GDR but after that date it became an exodus' [144: 186]. Prior to 16 November 1976, Biermann had not even been popular among his fellow countrymen; afterwards he was celebrated as 'a political martyr' [130: 120]. On balance, the SED Politburo's attempt to punish thought crime proved counterproductive. Once again the totalitarian regime had scored a pyrrhic victory.

Popular opinion

A key debate surrounding the 1970s is the extent to which Honecker stabilized the GDR by winning popular support for the regime. According to Madarász, East German society was 'viable' and 'supported by the majority of the population' [130: 192]. She even refers to 'the continuing acceptance of the political system' [130: 35]. Mitter and Wolle, on the other hand, postulate a trajectory of continuous decline caused by a state of latent civil war between rulers and ruled [152]. Both interpretations are inaccurate.

In 1993 Heinz Niemann claimed that the SED had successfully generated 'basic legitimacy and support for the regime in the 1970s' [130: 109]. He based his conclusions on surveys of the GDR's *Institut für Meinungsforschung* or Institute for Public Opinion Research [130: 109]. Yet such opinion data has to be handled with caution. The extent to which people were willing to state their real views in a dictatorship as strict as that of the SED is open to question. Similarly, when evaluating the poll findings of Professor Walter Friedrich's *Zentralinstitut für Jugendforschung* or Central Institute for Youth Research in Leipzig, it is important to remember that answers given were conditioned by the questions asked. Enquiring of young GDR citizens whether or not they supported their country, believed in Marxist-Leninism or had faith in the spread of socialism worldwide was clearly intended to elicit a certain response. In a state dedicated to blocking access to reliable information and bombarding its populace with propaganda, the idea that young people's views can be evaluated on the same basis as those living in more democratic societies is highly dubious. In 1975 Friedrich's researchers posed the question: 'Do you agree with the statement, "I am proud to be a citizen of our Socialist state"?' Fifty-seven per cent answered that they 'identified completely and 38 per cent did so with reservations. Only five per cent identified hardly or not at all' [26: 33]. But as Childs points out, 'youngsters are unlikely to be able to differentiate between the state and the community in which they live. To say they reject the state would be almost like saying they reject their country, town and friends' [26: 33]. Moreover, what young people were *not* asked is significant too. Had their views been sincerely sought on whether or not competitive elections should be held in the GDR, whether or not citizens should be allowed to travel freely to visit friends and relatives in the Federal Republic, or whether or not Germany should be reunited again, the answers – so long as they were freely given – might have been different. One can only agree with Childs that 'Friedrich's surveys were useful in showing the trend but probably greatly underestimated the doubts and disaffection which existed among GDR young people' [26: 33].

A further impression of public opinion can be gleaned from classified Stasi reports. In an opinion poll of factory employees in 1974, for example, '20.6 per cent of those questioned "considered that friendship with the USSR restricted the GDR's autonomy and brought more benefit to the Soviet Union than to the GDR"' [5: 354–55]. As for the catchphrase 'achieving working-class power', most felt unable to explain its meaning. More worryingly for the SED, some of the remarks on the slogan recorded in the report forwarded to the KGB were downright hostile. Given the understandable wariness of those questioned in uttering anti-party viewpoints, the true level of discontent is likely to have been much higher [5: 355].

Honecker certainly enjoyed a honeymoon period after coming to power. There was widespread popular appreciation of the additional welfare policies introduced during the 1970s. While Zatlin is right that 'the SED's economic paternalism increased its control over the economy', his claim that it did so 'without increasing popular support for communism' requires qualification [230: 54]. A key survey carried out in 1976 by the Institute for Public Opinion

Research reinforced its earlier conclusions. As Dennis points out, 'over three-quarters of the 4,777 respondents from 67 factories and institutions stated that basic material and social security was better in their country than in the West' [39: 157]. This data should be taken seriously because opinion polls conducted after the downfall of SED rule, when respondents felt less inhibited about expressing their views, showed strong backing for fundamental elements of a Socialist welfare state [39: 157]. East German citizens often defined their country by the issue of social security. A 1973 survey carried out 'among teachers on behalf of the Ministry for Education noted social security as the primary characteristic of the GDR' [130: 167]. Madarász argues that Honecker's approach 'helped to integrate great parts of the population, in particular women and to some extent young people, into the socialist society' [130: 172]. While integration did not usually translate into ideological agreement, it was still a significant advance on the 1950s and 1960s.

The generation that came of age in the 1970s had experienced neither the Weimar Republic nor National Socialism. They had therefore been socialized by the system to a greater extent than their parents. Certain foreign policy initiatives also presented the regime in a more positive light. In his autobiography, the GDR's spy-master Markus Wolf, remembers that Honecker's aid to Chilean and other Latin American left-wingers, who were being persecuted by right-wing dictatorships, proved popular with young people in the East: 'It is not an exaggeration to say that these campaigns in the 1970s strengthened East Germany by giving the beleaguered country a patina of respectability' [226: 345]. According to Wolle, GDR citizens were permitted to demonstrate 'spontaneously' against the 1973 military coup in Chile [94: 150]. The 'Workers' and Peasants' State' never enjoyed anything approaching majority support but neither was it merely despised or tolerated by the population.

Most people grudgingly participated in the totalitarian dictatorship to get on in life and because they saw no prospect of its removal. Popular acceptance of SED rule, in so far as it existed, was conditional, selective and half-hearted. The party knew this. Evidence of its mistrust is the malignant growth of the Stasi. West Germany's increasingly successful 'social market economy' also necessitated further fortification of the Berlin Wall. Pulzer goes so far as to claim that 'discontent increased rather than diminished in the course of the 1970s, as memories of the heroic reconstruction period dimmed and the continuing hardships of everyday life were resented more strongly' [179: 106].

Perhaps the country's shallow basis in popular legitimacy is best illustrated by Honecker's abortive attempt to manufacture a new East German national identity during the 1970s [156; 165]. After 1974, the SED propagated the doctrine that the GDR had developed into a discrete Socialist nation which 'had little or nothing in common' with the FRG [26: 31]. Most East Germans, however, continued to feel part of a single German nation. Their access to West German radio and television undermined the party's attempts to insulate them from the West and exploded the myth of the GDR's superiority. East Germany was probably more stable during this period than in any other but, as Madarász herself concedes, it was 'a precarious stability' [130]. According to Allinson, 'had an international catalyst permitted regime change in the GDR in 1977, it seems certain that this opportunity would have been seized as willingly then as proved to be the case in 1989' [61: 276].

5 Crisis, 1977–89

The onset of crisis

Fulbrook has dated the start of East Germany's 'destabilization' to 1980 [58: 377]. In the view of Schroeder, the 'SED-State' entered its period of 'stagnation and crisis' in 1981 [196: 255]. Weber avers that the country's 'paralysis' commenced in 1982 [220: 178] and Steiner identifies that year as the beginning of the GDR's final phase [208: 171–96]. There are, however, four reasons for suggesting 1977–8 as the key turning point.

The first is the economy. Although East German citizens enjoyed the highest living standards in the Soviet bloc, problems were mounting. As a country with few natural resources, the GDR was hit hard by the sharp rise in raw material prices after the 1973 oil crisis [39: 161; 158: 141]. The SED was also borrowing heavily from the West to pay for its increased imports of consumer goods and expensive welfare policies. 'By 1977', argues Allinson, 'it was clear to many that the SED's early hopes of building a strong economy were unravelling' [61: 273]. In that year, a critical altercation took place between Honecker and his two principal economic aides, Günter Mittag, Central Committee Secretary for the Economy, and Gerhard Schürer, Chairman of the State Planning Commission [230: 78]. They tried to convince him of the need to address the burgeoning debt problem. According to their calculations, there would be a shortfall of 1.7 billion marks in 1978 [26: 25]. But Honecker rejected their analysis because it entailed the introduction of an austerity programme, which threatened to reduce living standards and destabilize the regime politically [230: 79].

The Soviet Union could not afford to increase its subsidies. East Germany's 'net external debt with the West almost doubled between 1977 and 1981, reaching in the latter year US$10.1 billion with the OECD countries, excluding the FRG' [39: 162]. Its cumulative trade deficit with the Federal Republic rose to 3.7 billion marks over the same period [39: 162]. The regime had to devise desperate means of obtaining hard currency from the West. These included 'appropriating the funds of Christian religious institutions, prostituting East German women, and selling political prisoners to the Federal Republic' [230: 93]. Yet Honecker persisted with his ruinous policies until October 1989. As Allinson concludes, 'there was an acute sense during 1977 that things were getting worse, not better, and that difficulties on the ground were clearly linked to systemic factors' [61: 274].

The second reason is the informal church–state agreement of 6 March 1978, in which the SED recognized that religion – contrary to Marxist theory – was not about to disappear soon. Among other concessions, the Protestant Churches were granted controlled access to GDR radio and television, pension entitlements for clergy, reparation for confiscated property, authorization to establish new churches on condition they were paid for by the FRG, and the right to import ecclesiastical literature from the West [25: 443; 39: 247]. This was interpreted by some as a deliberate, albeit limited, experiment in liberalization or pluralism. It was no such thing. The party's need to avoid public displays of repression in the era of *détente* and *Ostpolitik* prompted it to try to integrate the Protestant Churches. It also wanted to placate Christians before introducing mandatory military instruction for all 15- and 16-year-olds later that year [25: 443]. Perhaps an additional incentive was the crisis unleashed by the self-immolation of Pastor Oskar Brüsewitz in 1976, 'interpreted as a protest against the state's treatment of the church' [37: 178]. Despite the agreement, another self-immolation occurred on 17 September 1978, this time by an evangelical pastor called Rolf Günther [220: 325].

By permitting reliable clergy to attend convocations abroad, Honecker aimed to gain international recognition for the 'Workers' and Peasants' Power' while getting the clergy to speak for his policies [25: 443]. In order to build historical legitimacy for the 'Socialist nation', the SED set about manipulating aspects of German history it had previously condemned. The church–state 'concordat' was part of this strategy. In 1983, the party would celebrate the five-hundredth anniversary of Martin Luther's birth and the 'revolutionary' acts of Thomas Müntzer, the sixteenth-century

Anabaptist [25: 444]. That same year, Mielke's second-in-command, Rudi Mittig, affirmed: 'Religion is and remains a type of bourgeois ideology and is incompatible with Marxism–Leninism. At this particular time, such an assessment cannot be the subject of public discussion but it must always determine the political as well as the basic political–operative conception' [39: 248]. In other words, the SED had changed tactics but not its long-term objectives [39: 248].

Honecker felt confident enough to make 'the historic compromise of 6 March 1978' [59: 109] because the Protestant Churches were under Stasi surveillance. They would be subjected to even deeper penetration in the years to come [30]. According to a letter from Mielke to MfS officers on 19 April 1978, the aim was 'to subvert, divide and paralyse "hostile–negative" persons and groups' within their ranks [39: 247]. The main Evangelical Church had already been prevailed upon to separate from its West German counterparts in 1969. Subsequently, it had moved to accommodate rather than oppose the regime. As Bishop Albrecht Schönherr put it in 1971: 'We want to be a church not alongside, not against, but rather a church within socialism' [59: 106; 25: 442–3]. Finally, organized Christianity had been weakened by processes of secularization.

The regime's attempt to co-opt the Protestant Churches for the purpose of controlling dissent backfired disastrously, though. Its mistake was to presume that they worked according to the same centralizing principles as the SED, when in fact church leaders could not discipline 'turbulent priests' like Communist Party members [59: 116]. In their seminal study of totalitarianism, Friedrich and Brzezinski identify the churches as an 'island of separateness' in the totalitarian sea [54: 247–63]. Given their infiltration by the Stasi, those in the GDR are best characterized as heavily inundated, semi-submerged 'islands of separateness'. Throughout the 1980s, however, their flood defences were robust enough to provide embattled shelter for various peace, human rights, and environmentalist groups [59: 201–42] that formed within the interstices of ossified totalitarian structures. By rekindling the embers of civil society, these courageous men and women lit a flame which eventually ignited the conflagration of 1989 [145: 160]. Honecker's failure to turn the Protestant Churches into a long arm of the state marked the onset of a sclerosis that was to have disastrous consequences for the regime. To quote Fulbrook, the church–state agreement of 6 March 1978 'proved to be the beginning of the end' [59: 109].

The third reason why 1977–8 represents the start of the GDR's crisis is the introduction, on 1 September 1978, of compulsory military instruction in schools for all 15- and 16-year-olds. This provoked ecclesiastical hostility, which was expressed in a letter from the Conference of Governing Bodies of the Evangelical Churches to the parishes on 14 June [229: 185–92]. It was also an important factor in the church's formation of the unofficial peace movement, *Frieden schaffen ohne Waffen* or 'Create Peace Without Weapons' in 1980. The badge of the movement carried the biblical quotation, 'Swords into ploughshares', and was banned by the SED [26: 43]. Needless to say, the party favoured peace *with* weapons and saw no contradiction between peace and militarism in the 'Workers' and Peasants' State'. In its view, 'military instruction and the credibility of peace policies went hand in hand. The GDR's stability and readiness to defend itself had contributed decisively to preserving and securing peace in Central Europe' [229: 187]. The introduction of 'Socialist Military Education' demonstrated the heightened importance of ideology in Honecker's East Germany. Since the notion of an independent peace movement offended the regime's totalitarian pretensions, it was criminalized. But despite Stasi harassment, *Frieden schaffen ohne Waffen* continued to grow.

The fourth reason is the publication of a reform Communist 'manifesto' by the West German magazine, *Der Spiegel* (The Mirror), in January 1978. It had allegedly been written by a 'Democratic League of Communists', consisting of disaffected SED functionaries. The response of the regime was to close the magazine's office in East Berlin and arrest the author, who turned out to be an economist named Hermann von Berg. But his excoriating critique of the SED dictatorship proved prophetic. East Germany, he claimed, was economically bankrupt in 1977–8. Furthermore, it was run by a bloated, corrupt, and parasitical bureaucracy. As for the German question, it was still open [74: 161–85]. By 1977–8, the GDR was already slipping into crisis. Von Berg was one of the first to realize it. To quote Allinson again, '1977 marks something of a halfway point between the end of the cycle of events that established the GDR's new status in the international sphere and, arguably, the start of the sequence of internal events that contributed to the state's eventual dissolution' [61: 253].

The role of *Ostpolitik*

Ostpolitik survived not only the deterioration of Superpower relations in 1980 but also the collapse of Helmut Schmidt's Social Democrat–Liberal government in the FRG on 17 September 1982. Yet the original aim, according to Garton Ash, was largely abandoned in favour of maintaining peace and stability [69: 203–4]. In 1982–3 the GDR suffered a major liquidity crisis and had to be bailed out by the new centre-right coalition of Helmut Kohl in Bonn. A pivotal role was also played by Bavaria's staunchly anti-Communist Premier, Franz Josef Strauß. After German reunification, some protested that these credits had helped prolong the life of the beleaguered republic. But this is to misconstrue the historical context. East Germany's life was safe so long as it was protected by the Kremlin. In 1983 the Cold War was at its coldest and there was no prospect of the Soviet Union forsaking its German ally.

If the FRG had refused credit, two scenarios might have unfolded. First, the 'Workers' and Peasants' State' could have sunk deeper into crisis. This would have created a potentially dangerous situation between the Superpowers at a time when the threat of nuclear war seemed real. Second, Honecker might have been deposed by his SED comrades and a draconian austerity programme instituted. It is doubtful whether this would have 'strengthened the GDR', as Zatlin claims [230: 144–5]. The potential for civil unrest as living standards fell would have necessitated increased repression, intensifying human suffering and damaging the country's domestic and international prospects. Whatever the intentions of West German politicians, these loans made the GDR financially dependent on Bonn. They also brought the 'Workers' and Peasants' Power' to the brink of insolvency by 1989, further discrediting socialism in the eyes of the populace [230: 145].

In return for receiving credits in 1983 and 1984, Honecker eased restrictions on travel to West Germany and decommissioned the tripwire weapons along the frontier with the Federal Republic [230: 140–1]. This helped to loosen the Gordian knot of SED rule. The increasing numbers of East Germans attempting to leave the GDR was symptomatic of the worsening crisis. In 1980 there had been 21,500 applications to emigrate. The total rose each year, reaching 113,500 in 1988 [26: 44]. Surveys carried out in 1984 and 1989 show that emigrants were motivated slightly more by political considerations than material factors [39: 274]. Between 1949 and 1961 it had been the other way round.

Despite the demise of *détente* following the Soviet invasion of Afghanistan on 27 December 1979, the SED leadership came to believe good-neighbourly relations with West Germany would facilitate rather than impede its quest for domestic legitimacy [142: 197–8]. The crowning moment of Honecker's career was his state visit to the Federal Republic between 7 and 11 September 1987. Yet according to the Stasi, young East Germans understood it to mean that the Berlin Wall and the concept of 'West German imperialism' were both anachronistic [40: 222]. When Honecker made his celebrated remarks in Bonn that 'socialism and capitalism can no more be combined than fire and water' [69: 172], he had no idea that the fires of communism would soon be extinguished by a flood of revolution. The prestige bestowed on the GDR by his visit eclipsed the domestic crisis and lulled him into a false sense of security [75: 214]. In the long run, the fruits of *Ostpolitik* proved poisonous for the regime.

Systemic sclerosis

A totalitarian polity can be compared to an individual who tries to control every detail in his or her life, thereby running the risk of suffering a nervous breakdown. The SED was hoist with its own petard, its obsessive-compulsive urge to direct an increasingly complex society eventually leading to 'bureaucratic overstretch' and multiple sclerosis of the body politic. Needless to say, regimes that seek to control everything can also expect to be blamed for everything. By discriminating against political dissidents in the field of employment, the party 'politicized' and 'professionalized' the East German opposition [110: 174]. It is the view of Dennis that: 'While the Stasi could congratulate itself on keeping the lid on the opposition groups, it was suppressing a critical potential which might have rejuvenated the GDR, and left it better prepared to face the challenges of unification and transformation' [40: 245]. Ultimately, the MfS undermined support for the 'Workers' and Peasants' Power' because most of the population perceived it 'as a hostile element' [28: 177].

With regard to the environment, untold damage was done by the regime's one-size-fits-all methodology and fear of 'complexity, diversity and the individual' [158: 186]. As Nelson has concluded: 'The lesson of East German forestry is that we should make policy with an eye toward reducing control to increase individual freedom and autonomy and let communities emerge from the bottom up' [158: 185]. For the GDR's economic planners, nature 'was there to be beaten into submission' [14: 323]. The resulting environmental degradation exposed the official half-truth that ecological problems were caused by capitalism, not socialism [14: 324].

A key debate among historians is whether the country's economic problems were systemic or more a result of unpropitious circumstances. Steiner contends that 'the crucial negative element was the planned-economy system' [208: 1]. In the view of Fulbrook, however, it is at least arguable whether 'the growing economic problems ... originated not so much in any non-viability of a centrally-planned economy in principle, as in the changing international economic situation and concomitant rising indebtedness in the GDR from the oil crises of 1973 onwards' [59: 172]. The truth is closer to Steiner's position. Although the title of his book, *The Plans that Failed*, understates the relative success of the East German economy during its first two decades, Fulbrook overlooks the fact that centrally-planned economies usually work only in underdeveloped or war-torn states. Built on the Soviet model of the 1930s, the GDR's totalitarian system mobilized resources for post-war reconstruction but was ill suited to the country's relatively advanced and diverse industrial base in the long run. When it came to delivering the goods for a consumer society, it proved far less effective than capitalism.

In other words, the republic's economic problems were increasingly systemic, although unfavourable circumstances certainly exacerbated the situation. The second 'oil shock' of 1979 prompted the USSR to slash its subsidized oil deliveries to East Germany and redirect them 'to hard currency markets in the West' [158: 141]. Apart from harming her economy, this had the effect of compelling the GDR to become dependent on its large reserves of lignite or 'brown coal' [158: 141]. By 1990, the country consumed an astronomical 40 per cent of the world's lignite production [158: 142]. The burning of this filthy substance caused severe environmental damage.

More fundamentally, the 'administrative-command system' [75: 57] failed to keep pace with the 'scientific-technological revolution' because it was designed for a 'hardware' not a 'software' economy [217: 498–9]. An overweening bureaucracy stifled initiative. In the 1980s, the General Director of Carl Zeiss, a 'People-Owned Enterprise', suggested to Günter Mittag that the Ministry of Science and Technology be wound up, since it did nothing more than impose 'bureaucratic reporting requirements' [133: 96]. What Delores Augustine calls the 'totalitarian impulse' was dramatically heightened during the Honecker years, as 'the Stasi and SED greatly increased their control over day-to-day technical and managerial decisions in high-tech industry' [6: 321, 327]. As political loyalty became the *sine qua non* for career advancement, 'competition to innovate was replaced by competition to be most politically correct' [6: 349]. Hence Honecker's new interest in the 'scientific-technological revolution', manifested in attempts to prioritize microelectronics and robot technology, came to nothing [151: 226]. Steiner maintains that 'the Socialist economic system's immanent incapacity to produce structural and technological or innovatory change was the decisive cause of the GDR's economic weakness in its final decade' [208: 193].

According to Maier, 'the disabling failures' set in during the early 1970s [133: 81]. His argument presupposes that a chance for reform was missed during that decade. Yet no such opportunity existed. The economies of Poland and Hungary were less totalitarian than East Germany's but ultimately fared no better. Certainly, the 1970s was a crucial decade. The world recession presented communism and capitalism with similar challenges [133: 81]. But the kind of painful restructuring carried out in the West was difficult to envisage within the confines of the GDR's rigid structures. Instead, the SED took refuge in what Kopstein calls a 'campaign economy' which 'doomed economic life in the GDR to a never-ending series of politically directed economic campaigns of extremely limited effectiveness' [114: 110].

Maier describes the resulting absurdities and contradictions in some detail: 'there were many deep-freezes but not enough foil wraps and containers. Wholesale houses produced 19 models of anoraks for children, but retail stores wouldn't buy them because they were penalized for having inventories in stock. Consumers always preferred the same few fragrances of room sprays ... but the factory continually had to change the assortment offered to attain its prescribed innovation ratio of 30 per cent' [133: 80].

Vinen recounts that 'when factory managers were given orders to install a certain quota of "robots" in all plants, they responded by redefining existing devices – such as lifts and vacuum cleaners – to fit this new category' [217: 499]. As supply problems became endemic during the 1980s, a growing black market was spawned. Most accounts identify price distortion as the source of scarcity in planned economies. But in a ground-breaking study, Jonathan Zatlin attributes it primarily to the regime's ideological antipathy towards money [230].

The smoke-belching Trabant, the legendary plastic car of the land, was emblematic of this systemic failure. Since the state did not subsidize them, Trabants 'were very expensive for most East Germans' [230: 225]. Waiting times could be more than 13 years, which meant that by 1989 a used 'Trabi' could cost nearly double the price of a new one [230: 227, 233]. The regime had an 'ideological distaste for producing cars' [230: 219], believing they constituted a 'false need' [230: 215]. Hence too few of them were manufactured. The SED's policy of dictating to the population what its consumer desires should be was self-defeating. The hapless 'vehicle of desire' [230: 203–42] was the butt of numerous jokes in East Germany. For example: 'Why have Sex-Shops not yet been established in the GDR? Because driving a Trabi is more effective than any vibrator' [41: 105]. Another went: 'Why are there no bank robbers in the GDR? Because one has to wait ten years for a getaway car!' [41: 106]. The sight of Trabis streaming West in 1989 presaged the downfall of the 'Workers' and Peasants' State'.

As for the party's social policies, they had signally failed to boost productivity. Instead they raised expectations that could not be fulfilled. East Germans used their increased wages and leisure time to do more shopping, thus exacerbating supply shortages. Honecker's welfare programmes became unaffordable. This was disastrous for the SED because they were integral to its claims on legitimacy [190: 96]. While in 1970 subsidies had amounted to eight billion marks per year, by 1989 the cost had soared to a crippling 58 billion marks per annum, 'outpacing by almost two to one the growth in national product' [26: 26]. Combined social expenditure on consumer price subsidies, housing, education, health and social welfare, as well as social insurance amounted to 112.3 billion marks in 1985. Five years earlier the total had been 72.9 billion marks [37: 165].

The Polish crisis of 1980–1 had shown how quickly social discontent could degenerate into political unrest [196: 255]. Unable to cut welfare spending, Mittag withheld desperately-needed capital from the GDR's industrial infrastructure, further undermining the country's competitiveness [230: 324]. Upon discovering the scale of the debt in May 1989, Honecker's deputy, Egon Krenz, exclaimed: 'For me there is no question whether the unity of economic and social policy should be continued. It must be continued because it *is* socialism in the GDR!' [190: 96] Thus the main cause of the gathering crisis was the totalitarian welfare state itself.

East Germany's government employed a vast and expensive 'double' bureaucracy to plan all aspects of societal life. In this dual structure of party and state, the former supervised the latter, duplicating many of its functions in the process [56: 19–20]. As Dennis points out, the party's elite functionaries alone 'numbered between 300,000 and 400,000, that is about three per cent of the adult population. But this was just the tip of the political and administrative iceberg' [39: 197]. SED leaders frequently criticized bureaucratic behaviour but failed to perceive that the problem was systemic.

The best illustration of the link between totalitarian control and rampant bureaucracy is the Stasi. Just prior to the fall of the Berlin Wall in 1989, the MfS employed 91,105 full-time functionaries and approximately 176,000 IMs [40: 6] to oversee a population of 16.4 million [40: 4]. Dennis has calculated that 'in any given year throughout the 1980s, about one in 50 of the country's 13.5 million adults were working for the Stasi on the home front, either as an officer or as an informer' [40: xi]. According to Koehler, 'when one adds in the estimated numbers of part-time snoops, the result is nothing short of monstrous: one informer per 6.5 citizens' [112: 9]. The ratio of state security employees to population was 1:180 in the GDR (MfS), 1:595 in the USSR (KGB), 1:867 in Czechoslovakia (StB) and 1:1,574 in Poland (SB) in 1989–90 [48: 341]. Mielke's dystopian aim, already stated in the late 1940s, was 'to know everything and to report on everything worth knowing' [40: 23]. His ministry even collected the personal smells of its victims [70: 16]. To quote Koehler again: 'East German Communist leaders saturated their realm with more spies than had any other totalitarian government in recent history' [112: 8–9]. In the opinion of Childs and Popplewell, it can be argued that the Stasi 'came very near to its leaders' desire to know everything worth knowing about their own population and about the outside world' [28: xiii].

This Orwellian quest for omniscience required an outlay which the GDR could ill afford. The Stasi's budget remained a state secret until 1990. In 1989 it was said to have been roughly four billion marks a year [59: 48]. Then there was the problem of information overload. The MfS left behind approximately six million paper files [112: 20] and archival holdings running to 185 kilometres [40: 7]. Its 'intellectual property' stretched 'to tens of thousands of kilometres of documentation and tapes' [40: 243]. Yet, as Bruce points out, the Stasi's destruction of its own material after the fall of the Wall means the amount collected was far greater [23: 3]. Over 40 years, according to Anna Funder, '"the Firm" generated the equivalent of all records in German history since the middle ages' [65: 5]. Fixated on details, it completely failed to foresee the demise of communism or the country itself [65: 5]. Mitter and Wolle are right to argue that the 'bloated, inefficient and expensive Stasi apparatus harmed the GDR more than all the opposition groups put together' [152: 538]. In the view of Dennis, the organization suffered from 'the paradox of omnipotence' [40: 12].

The costs of the Berlin Wall and the NVA were also prohibitive. The GDR's principal economic historian, Jürgen Kuczynski, claimed that if the government halted expenditure on arms in the late 1970s it could provide East Germans 'with free gas and electricity' and 'introduce a 35-hour working week' [37: 185]. The problem was compounded by the demise of *détente* in 1980 and the concomitant refreezing of Superpower relations. According to the International Institute for Strategic Studies, the GDR's defence expenditure in 1984 'was 7.7 per cent of national income compared with four per cent for Czechoslovakia, the next highest spender of the Warsaw Pact (excluding the Soviet Union)' [26: 26].

Communist leaders remained imprisoned in an ideological mindset forged during the Weimar years [222: 5, 17, 386; 47: 262, 264–5]. They came to be blinded by their own propaganda, inhabiting an 'ideal' or a 'perfect world' ('*heile Welt*'), as the historian Stefan Wolle has convincingly argued [228: 121]. In 1986, Honecker insisted that GDR citizens lived in one of the freest countries on the planet [220: 197]. On 1 December 1988 he even went so far as to aver that 'basically' the standard of living in East Germany was 'higher' than that of the Bonn Republic [220: 186]. Politburo member Günter

Schabowski would later testify that he did not begin to clear his head of 'Marxist–Leninist rubbish' until 1990 [153: 35]. Ideology, a key feature of totalitarianism, played a crucial role in the party leadership until the end.

The heavily varnished reports sent to the centre by district and local party officials only fortified the rarefied fool's paradise in which party leaders cocooned themselves. Most functionaries dared not submit truthful reports lest they be blamed for the problems identified within them. In 1988 and 1989, almost all failed to inform the Politburo accurately of the deteriorating situation in the country at large. In this sense, ideology served a powerful 'blocking function' [71: 137]. As Krenz told Honecker in 1989, 'Do you really believe that we failed because the people were incapable? Among other reasons, we failed because we did not really live among the people, because we constructed a world of illusions (*Scheinwelt*). The information that we received was varnished (*geschönt*)' [56: 17]. Moreover, as Dennis has pointed out, 'the SED's strict adherence to an ideologically-based interpretation of how the Capitalist West would act meant that intelligence information which ran against the political grain was often ignored' [40: 209]. The prism of Marxist–Leninism exaggerated 'the steering influence of Western "imperialists"' [40: 209] and over-simplified the manifestations of dissent in the GDR. According to Mampel, the MfS served as the SED's 'ideology police'. It was well informed about conditions in East Germany but laboured under a 'fantasy' of 'political–ideological diversion' [56: 37–52]. While the Stasi served as a long pair of ears for the party, the space between them often proved rather limited.

Not only was reality distorted by ideology and propaganda; the state's monopoly on the means of communication prevented reliable information from being made available to those who needed it. Its occupation of the public sphere, together with its manufacturing of consent, prevented the bureaucracy from identifying real problems and tackling them rationally [56: 18]. This manufactured consent took many forms, the most notable of which were the orchestration of sham elections; 'acclamations' and stage-managed popular 'demonstrations'; 'discussion contributions written in advance'; and 'letters to newspaper editors written by the Stasi' [56: 17–18]. Meanwhile, the chasm between an increasingly restive society and the stifling party-state 'reached monumental proportions' [222: 387]. Freedom of expression is the oxygen of political life. Yet this oxygen, like so much else in the GDR, was strictly rationed. Consequently, the state organism went into a coma. Ultimately, only the Soviet leader could switch off the life-support machine.

Existential crisis: the impact of Gorbachev's reforms

East Germany's besetting problems were thrown into sharp relief by Mikhail Gorbachev's appointment as CPSU General Secretary on 12 March 1985. His policies of *glasnost* ('openness') and *perestroika* ('restructuring') were meant to rejuvenate the Socialist Motherland but ended up undermining the whole 'Socialist Commonwealth'. Crushed by the burden of Cold War defence expenditure, the Soviet empire had become overstretched. The Kremlin therefore decided that its military presence in Eastern Europe diminished rather than strengthened USSR security, and at a CPSU Central Committee plenum in February 1988, Gorbachev conceded 'the right of every people and every country to "choose freely its social and political system"' [75: 164]. Naturally, at this time he still believed that reform Communist governments would replace the discredited totalitarian regimes in the region. He also made clear that every Communist Party enjoyed full sovereignty [75: 169]. Consequently, the leadership of the 'Workers' and Peasants' State' was able to eschew reform.

Gorbachev's desire for disarmament provoked acrimonious debate in the SED Politburo. The party's ideological spokesman, Kurt Hager, worried that unilateral action by Communist countries would destabilize the GDR and Eastern Europe. Gorbachev went ahead regardless, announcing Soviet troop withdrawals at the United Nations on 7 December 1988 and anticipating reductions in the NVA a month later [75: 170–1]. Even more galling for East Berlin was Moscow's increasing acceptance that, irrespective of the existence of two German states, there was only one German nation [75: 178].

For the SED leadership, reform in the GDR was at best unnecessary and at worst destructive. Honecker believed he had already carried out sufficient 'restructuring' on taking over from Ulbricht in 1971. The first tensions between East Berlin and Moscow surfaced at the SED's 11th Party Congress in April 1986, where Gorbachev was somewhat critical of the East Germans' failure to decentralize the economy [190: 131]. On 9 April 1987, in an interview with the West German magazine *Stern* (Star), Hager made the SED Politburo's hostility to the reform process in the USSR abundantly clear. If your neighbour changes the wallpaper in his apartment, he asked, would you feel obliged to do the same? [108: 445]. Honecker's determination to resist democratic reform has sometimes been blamed for his country's demise. In the 1970s, the political dissident, Robert Havemann, wrote that 'freedom' had become a 'necessity' for socialism [229: 164–5]. Yet, as a precarious Cold War state bordering the magnetic Federal Republic, East Germany was congenitally incapable of sustaining liberalization. Paradoxically, then, totalitarianism was both the lifeblood and the wasting disease of the GDR.

Although the SED leadership did not dare to lambaste the reformers in Moscow publicly, it did its best to insulate the GDR against the disruptive neighbour two doors down. On 20 October 1987 the Politburo passed a resolution stipulating that in future the speeches of Soviet leaders would be censored before being published in East Germany [155: 17]. Over the next two years, it took the unprecedented step of proscribing Soviet articles, journals, and films. In November 1988, the German-language edition of the Soviet news digest, *Sputnik*, which advocated liberalization, vanished from the kiosks [119: 520]. The October edition had dared to contend that the KPD was partly responsible for the rise of the Nazis between 1932 and 1933 because of its dogmatic refusal to ally with the SPD. This offended a regime that presented itself as anti-fascist [190: 131]. Incredibly, 'it was now easier to get contemporary Soviet publications in West Berlin than in East Berlin' [119: 520]. Copies of Gorbachev's speeches began to fetch high prices on the black market. SED censorship proved counterproductive, however, since it intensified cravings for the forbidden fruits of *glasnost*. Following the prohibition of *Sputnik* on 18 November 1988, the SED was bombarded with furious letters of protest, some of them from party members [145: 165].

As fraternal relations with the bigger brother deteriorated, the SED leadership began pointing up 'national peculiarities' in East Germany's development, even coining the slogan 'socialism in the colours of the GDR' [220: 197] to highlight its independence.

The GDR leaders were terrified that their captive population would be infected by the democratic virus emanating from Moscow [145: 166]. They were right to be worried. As Clay Large points out, 'East Germans began demonstrating for reforms similar to those being undertaken in the Soviet Union; when challenged by the police, they flashed Soviet badges and pictures of Gorbachev' [119: 520]. On 8 June 1987 crowds of young people gathered at the Brandenburg Gate in order to listen to a rock concert taking place on the other side of the Berlin Wall. The police, however, moved in and there were violent clashes [220: 338]. The young fans called out 'Gorby! Gorby!' and 'the Wall must go!' On 17 January 1988 more than 100 peace and human rights activists were arrested when they attended the officially sanctioned demonstration to honour Karl Liebknecht and Rosa Luxemburg, the assassinated leaders of the abortive Communist uprising in Berlin in 1919. They carried home-made banners emblazoned with Luxemburg's motto 'freedom is always freedom for dissenters'. Some of those detained were expelled from the GDR [220: 193–4, 340].

Even more terrifying for the Politburo was the prospect that elements inside the SED would start clamouring for liberalization. After all, the Communist Party was the linchpin of the totalitarian system, so any divisions within its ranks could destabilize the whole edifice [145: 166]. It is a common misconception that there was a clear dichotomy between the party and the people in the GDR. Some East German Communists were as enthusiastic, if not more so, than their fellow-countrymen about reform in the Soviet Union [152: 508–9]. Others, however, were much more critical. In 1988, the SED started some 23,000 proceedings against its own comrades, the highest number since 1946 [130: 193].

For the majority of East Germans, Gorbachev had come to personify hope and freedom. Opinion data collated by the country's Central Institute for Youth Research based in Leipzig shows that at the end of 1988, 83 per cent of those young people questioned declared a positive attitude towards Gorbachev, 50 per cent a very positive attitude. The figures for non-party members were 82 per cent and 49 per cent, for SED members 90 per cent and 55 per cent, respectively. Even more worrying for the Politburo was the finding that in early 1989 a mere eight per cent of non-Communist youth identified with the policies of the SED whereas only 48 per cent of young comrades professed to 'fully identify' with their party

[155: 46–7]. Clearly, developments in the Soviet Union were undermining confidence in the SED and encouraging East Germany's disaffected youth to speak out more freely. With the advent of Gorbachev, one teenager testified, 'we began to think' [117: 468]. Worse still from the regime's point of view, Gorbachev's policies were causing a precipitous decline in loyalty to the GDR among this generation. According to data from the Central Institute for Youth Research, 51 per cent professed to identify completely with their country in 1985. But in 1988, the year democracy began to develop in the USSR, those who claimed to identify completely fell from 28 per cent in May to 18 per cent in October [26: 33].

The coming of Gorbachev rendered East Germany's crisis existential. As Madarász has noted, 'Gorbachev's reforms challenged most of the basic assumptions of life in the GDR and questioned the validity of compromises that had supported the relationship between state and society for many years. They undermined the status quo and encouraged parts of the population to discuss more openly issues that had been taboo for many years – issues lethal to the stability of the state such as the lack of economic success, travel outside the Eastern bloc, and popular input into politics' [130: 193]. By early 1989 the Soviet neighbour had done much more than just change his wallpaper; in the name of building a new 'common European house' he had begun demolishing his apartment. The damage to the surrounding flats in the Communist 'block' would prove irreparable [145: 167].

6 Collapse, 1989–90

The end begins

The *annus mirabilis* of 1989 got off to an inauspicious start when, on 18 January, Honecker proclaimed that the Berlin Wall 'will still be standing in 50 or 100 years, if the reasons for its existence have not been removed' [211: 592–3]. As if to emphasize the point, border guards shot dead 20-year-old barman Chris Gueffroy as he tried to escape to West Berlin on the night of 5–6 February. Chris was about to be conscripted into the NVA but wanted no part in defending a state he detested. Instead, he yearned to travel abroad, particularly to the United States. His death unleashed a storm of international protest, prompting the SED General Secretary to revoke, albeit secretly, the 'shoot-to-kill' order in April [211: 588–90]. Hence Gueffroy became the last person to die this way. Honecker himself seemed blissfully unaware of the profound midlife crisis that plagued his beloved 'workers' and peasants' paradise'. He would soon discover that the existential danger came not from the Capitalist devil but from the guardian angels in Moscow.

On 7 May the GDR held local elections, which were judged to be even more fraudulent than usual by the opposition groups that observed them. Afterwards, small demonstrations took place in several places and 'hundreds of complaints' were lodged against the authorities [220: 211]. A few days earlier, on 2 May, Hungary, now under reform Communist rule, had begun to dismantle the Iron Curtain along its frontier with Austria [175: 544]. East German holidaymakers soon besieged the embassy of the Federal Republic in Budapest, hoping to gain permission to travel there. The embassies in Prague and Warsaw were also occupied. Then, on 10 and 11 September, without any prior consultation with its East German ally, Hungary permitted all GDR refugees to leave for the West, thereby causing the largest exodus from the 'Workers' and Peasants' State' since the building of the Berlin Wall [145: 167]. On 4 and 5 October, Czechoslovakia and Poland followed suit [220: 343–4]. SED leaders responded by closing their country's frontier with Czechoslovakia. The border with Poland stayed open but it was troublesome to traverse, even with a visa [26: 68].

Meanwhile, in the GDR's second largest city of Leipzig, Pastor Christian Führer was organizing prayers for peace at the city's *Nikolaikirche*. In a resulting demonstration on 11 September there were mass arrests. Arguably, this marked the beginning of the country's revolution. The arrests only inflamed the situation and every Monday more and more people took to the streets of the city to protest. Between late August and early October, a spate of new opposition groups was founded in East Germany, ranging from New Forum, Democracy Now, and Democratic Awakening to the Social Democratic Party in the GDR (SDP) [145: 167]. All pleaded for peaceful dialogue with the authorities. As the Stasi recognized, discontent was almost as prevalent among party members as among the population at large [220: 217].

Revolution

An important debate among historians is whether or not the seismic events of 1989–90 in the GDR – referred to as a '*Wende*' or 'change' – can be classified as a 'revolution'. Three interpretations have been advanced: 'revolution from below', 'implosion from within' and 'collapse from outside' [190: 126–48], all of which are based on a false or incomplete notion of what revolution actually entails.

Revolution is best defined as sudden systemic change. Within the space of 12 short months a political, economic and social system known as 'communism' was obliterated [145: 157], along with an entire way of life. This, then, was a social as well as a political revolution. Furthermore, unlike other East European countries, a 40-year-old state ceased to exist, its inhabitants joining the Capitalist-democratic FRG [145: 157]. In doing so, they immediately exchanged member-ship of the Warsaw Pact and Comecon for NATO and the European Community, respectively. A more dramatic transformation could hardly have been envisaged. Never before in history had two such different societies been merged in such a short period of time.

All this was achieved through the exertion of popular pressure on a dysfunctional system, through either the process of emigration ('exit') or that of demonstration ('voice'). The notion of 'systems failure', so prevalent among West German social scientists [190: 130], tells only part of the story. As Gareth Dale has observed, the 'state crisis and the burgeoning of social movements were mutually enhancing processes' [36: 224]. To emphasize one over the other, as some scholars have done, is to draw a false dichotomy.

Between September and December 1989, 'a constant, countrywide, almost simultaneous awakening took place ... in which two million people actively participated' [15: 28]. This amounted to more than 12 per cent of the population. Since the overwhelming majority of demonstrators were adults, the true percentage of active participants was even higher. As the GDR opposition activist, Bärbel Bohley, rightly claims, 'it was the largest democratic movement in German history so far', the equivalent of about 30 million people taking to the streets in the United States [15: 28, 30]. According to Judt, it 'was perhaps the only truly popular – i.e. mass – revolution of that year' [103: 616]. The movements elsewhere in Eastern Europe were mostly confined to the capital cities and a few other major towns [15: 28]. Only in Czechoslovakia might there have been greater popular participation. However, without the fall of the Berlin Wall, the 'Velvet Revolution' in the CSSR may not have happened. In Poland, Hungary, and Czechoslovakia, the transition to post-communism was more a process of negotiation between the Communist Parties and their respective oppositions [103: 616]. All things considered, the East German *Wende* was the most revolutionary of the 1989 Revolutions.

Peaceful revolution

The *Wende* has gone down in history as a peaceful affair [28: 193]. This is sometimes cited as evidence of its non-revolutionary nature. While the outcome was certainly gentle by the standards of previous revolutions, it should not be forgotten that countless citizens were arrested, beaten up, and manhandled by the security forces. In front of Dresden main station on 4 October 1989, 3,000 people clashed with a sizeable police force, supported by units of the NVA [119: 522].

Many in the crowd were trying to jump on one of the special GDR trains carrying 7,600 East German refugees from Czechoslovakia to the FRG. In an assertion of sovereignty, Honecker had insisted that they cross the territory of the German Democratic Republic [220: 215, 344], enabling him to confiscate their identification papers and formally deport them. The security services 'beat back the would-be-escapees with clubs' [119: 522]. Not one of them managed to board the train, 'but one young man fell under the wheels and lost both legs' [119: 522]. Next day, the security forces forcibly broke up mass demonstrations in Dresden and Magdeburg. On 6 and 7 October, as the 'Workers' and Peasants' State' celebrated its 40th birthday, large but peaceful demonstrations in numerous towns, including East Berlin, were violently dispersed [220: 216, 344; 152: 487]. Terms such as 'velvet revolution' hardly do justice to such episodes.

Only in Leipzig on 9 October, almost a month after the revolution had started, did 'the security forces show restraint for the first time' [220: 344]. The so-called 'miracle of Leipzig' [148: 200] marked an important turning point in that the regime's totalitarian monopoly on the means of coercion ceased to function. This further swelled the numbers of demonstrators. As a consequence, the system began to implode. Even then, however, the revolution was not completely free of violence. In East Berlin on 15 January 1990, tens of thousands stormed the former headquarters of the Stasi, the city's Bastille. They laid waste to it in the process. In response, the so-called Round Table, a discussion body containing representatives of the regime and the civil rights movement, issued an appeal for calm [220: 348]. Kettenacker's assertion that the 1989 Revolution in the GDR was 'totally peaceful' therefore requires qualification [107].

That said, the revolution did not result in a massacre, which was how the People's Republic of China celebrated its 40th birthday that year. There were four reasons for this. Most important was Gorbachev's refusal to countenance violence. In contrast to 17 June 1953, Soviet tanks did not roll [145: 169]. Despite the opposition of his own military, he had begun withdrawing troops from Afghanistan on 18 May 1988 [117: 33]. This was the beginning of the end for the Soviet empire. The last soldiers left in February 1989 following a decade of armed conflict. A bloodbath in the GDR was therefore anathema to the Kremlin. As Timothy Garton Ash observed: 'In East Germany, Moscow not only made it plain to the leadership that Soviet troops were not available for purposes of domestic repression, but also, it seems, went out of its way to let it be known – to the West, but also to the population concerned – that this was its position' [71: 141]. This sapped the morale of the GDR authorities.

The second factor relates to splits in the SED, not only within the leadership, but at regional level. These paralysed the party's decision-making capacity. By replacing the 77-year-old Honecker with Egon Krenz as SED General Secretary on 18 October 1989, the Politburo signalled that it had decided definitively against the use of force [145: 169]. The East German government had worked tirelessly to achieve international recognition and did not want to lose the associated benefits. A massacre in East Berlin could have jeopardized financial credits from Bonn, a benefit of *Ostpolitik*. According to Krenz's deputy, Wolfgang Herger, there was one principal reason why there had been no carnage in Leipzig on 9 October: 'Honecker knew that he would not have got the order through even if he had given it. It was too late to unite the leadership behind such action' [148: 201]. Party leaders in the city therefore lacked guidance from their superiors. In this terrifyingly uncertain situation, Kurt Masur, the conductor of Leipzig's famous '*Gewandhaus* orchestra', joined with three district SED secretaries to issue an appeal for non-violence – 'the first time that local functionaries had spoken out against the use of force to quell the demonstrations' [148: 200]. This might have influenced decision-making in East Berlin [148: 200–1].

Third, some members of the country's army, police and Combat Groups of the Working Class were unwilling to open fire on civilians, thereby weakening the power of the state at the crucial moment [108: 459]. Fourth, the tactics of the revolutionary crowds themselves were anything but provocative. Armed with nothing more than candles, they hardly fitted the description of rampaging counter-revolutionary mobs that the security forces had been trained to subdue [145: 169]. Their behaviour was driven mainly by fear of a regime crackdown, although the churches also played a constructive role.

Even so, this relatively peaceful outcome was by no means pre-ordained. As Childs and Popplewell acknowledge, 'one false move on the part of the opposition might have lead to civil war' [28: 190]. On 4 June 1989 the Chinese army had massacred students demonstrating for reform in Beijing's Tiananmen Square. Four days later, the GDR's parliament issued a statement praising the suppression of the 'counter-revolution' there [220: 343]. If there were any doubts about the East German regime's determination to put down similar disturbances at home, Margot Honecker, the hard-line Education Minister and wife of the SED General Secretary, dispelled them. At the Ninth Pedagogical Congress in June 1989, she condemned those advocating change in Eastern Europe as 'counter-revolutionaries' who wanted a restoration of capitalism. She then threatened violence: 'We are now in a period of struggle which needs young people who are willing to fight to strengthen socialism ... if necessary, with a rifle in their hands' [75: 170]. On 8 October, Mielke put the GDR's security forces on red alert [59: 253–4]. Two days later, Honecker welcomed an eminent Chinese official and mentioned the parallels between the 'counter-revolution' in Beijing and the disturbances in his own country. He then began preparing to crush the next Leipzig demonstration with methods not dissimilar to those deployed in China four months previously [33: 394]. Since the police were overwhelmed by the large numbers of protesters, Honecker issued a command to supply the NVA 'with live ammunition' [75: 175]. There must have been many in the security forces prepared to use it if called upon to do so. In Leipzig, 'hospitals were told to prepare blood reserves and body bags' [148: 201]. The 50,000 citizens who joined the demonstration on 9 October feared they might be marching into a massacre. For this reason the metropolis became known as 'the city of heroes' [148: 200]. That violence did not break out by accident was partly down to good luck. As late as 16 October, Mielke directed that the security services should deploy force if individuals or buildings were assaulted [28: 190].

The fall of the Berlin Wall

The fortuitous opening of the Berlin Wall on Thursday 9 November 1989 gave the revolution a huge impetus. It happened only because at an evening press conference, Politburo member Günter Schabowski forgot to mention that the new decree giving GDR citizens the right to an exit visa at any border crossing, including that of Berlin, applied merely to the country's four million passport holders. It was said to have been endorsed, albeit unofficially, by Gorbachev. Asked when the new regulations would take effect, Schabowski replied, 'immediately, without delay', instead of 10 November, as envisaged. The announcement triggered a rush of people to the Wall [133: 160–1]. Bereft of any guidance from the state's paralysed leadership, the local guards opened the border on their own initiative. In so doing, they played a major role in preventing a bloodbath. There followed one of the greatest spontaneous street parties in world history, as East and West Berliners exulted in their new-found unity. Over the next four days, 25 per cent of the GDR's population crossed the frontier [153: 301]. For many it was a moment of epiphany. In November alone, more than 133,000 refugees fled to the West, almost 90,000 of them after the Wall came down; 281,000 more would leave between December 1989 and the end of June 1990 [117: 459]. The fall of this most potent symbol of Communist oppression made 9 November 'the happiest day in the country's history' [148: 209]. However, McElvoy's claim that it was also its death knell neglects the decisive importance of Gorbachev [148: 209].

Once the so-called anti-fascist protective rampart had been breached, demonstrators stopped calling for the reform of East Germany and began demanding its abolition. Instead of 'We Are The People', they roared 'We Are *One* People!' Dale shows that popular protest did not go into terminal decline after 9 November, as some historians have claimed. On the contrary, the number of demonstrations and demonstrators in January 1990 easily surpassed those in October 1989. He concludes that 'while the movement did indeed peak in early November, it revived only a fortnight later, surged in early December, and crested yet again in mid-January' [36: 129]. Meanwhile the SED began to implode, as its functionaries lost the will to rule and the unshackled media reported stories of corruption at the highest levels. On 10 November 1989, the Central Committee adopted an action programme, which promised free-and-secret general elections. Then, on 13 November, the reform Communist Hans Modrow replaced Willi Stoph as Prime Minister of the GDR [220: 345]. On 1 December, a reinvigorated parliament deleted the party's 'leading role' from the country's constitution and the SED called an extraordinary Party Congress to begin the task of shedding its totalitarian baggage. Soon it had renamed itself the Party of Democratic Socialism (PDS). Krenz resigned as General Secretary on 3 December, along with the entire Politburo and Central Committee. On the same day, 'Erich Honecker and 11 other leading functionaries were expelled from the SED' [220: 346].

The 'Gorbachev factor'

A critical debate is whether external or internal factors were more important in the GDR's downfall. Here we can make a useful distinction between the *failure* of East Germany and its *collapse*. Its *failure* can partly be attributed to indigenous factors. Its *collapse*, however, could occur only once the Soviet Union had withdrawn its support. The 'Gorbachev factor' was particularly powerful in the GDR because the state was more dependent than its Warsaw Pact allies on the USSR [71: 65]. Martin McCauley was right to affirm in the early 1980s that 'only the collapse of Soviet willpower to defend the GDR could undermine it' [144: 4].

Gorbachev made the 1989 Revolution possible. At a Warsaw Pact summit in Bucharest between 7 and 8 July 1989, he buried the already defunct Brezhnev Doctrine, which legitimized Soviet interference in the internal affairs of its Socialist satellites [69: 634]. Satellite governments would now be accountable to their own populations and not to Moscow. On 25 October 1989, the Soviet Foreign Ministry's spokesman, Gennady Gerasimov, christened the new policy the 'Sinatra Doctrine' after the American crooner's song *My Way* [71: 140].

By permitting Hungary and Poland to liberalize, Gorbachev showed East Germans that emancipation from Moscow would be tolerated [145: 171]. He also refused to block Hungary's decision to open its border with Austria, thereby plunging the GDR into a refugee crisis. His prescient warning to the SED leadership at the GDR's 40th anniversary celebrations that 'life punishes those who come too late' [26: 69] amounted to a rejection of the totalitarian system, since it conceded that life controlled politics rather than the other way round. To add insult to injury, he denied Honecker the traditional comradely bear hug [33: 394]. Gorbachev even seemed to encourage the demonstrators: 'If you want democracy, take it and it will be yours' [75: 174]. In so doing, he discredited all SED propaganda about 'democracy' in the 'Workers' and Peasants' State' [75: 174]. 'Gorby mania' gripped not just the protestors but also the putatively loyal FDJ members who marched in East Berlin's official torchlight procession on 7 October. When the FRG magazine, *Der Spiegel*, conducted a public opinion survey in December, it found that Gorbachev was 'more popular' in the GDR 'than any of the German politicians, East or West' [26: 108–9]. On 9–10 November 1989 he had retrospectively endorsed the opening of the Berlin Wall. All things taken together, nobody destabilized the GDR as much as Gorbachev did.

Of course, in the autumn of 1989 the Soviet leader did not yet envisage giving up the GDR, only reforming it. At their meeting in Moscow on 1 November, Gorbachev and the new SED General Secretary, Egon Krenz, agreed that German reunification was 'not on the agenda' [220: 345]. The former believed that 'really existing socialism', although deeply flawed, was capable of sustaining democratization. It was this grand miscalculation that sent the system racing into history. Gorbachev's Communist Reformation ended up destroying the political religion it was supposed to save. When the East German Revolution developed a pro-Western dynamic, the Soviet leader refused to crush it, thereby ensuring its success. On 10 and 11 February 1990, West German Chancellor Helmut Kohl visited Moscow with his Foreign Minister, Hans-Dietrich Genscher. It was here that Gorbachev gave the 'green light' to reunification [69: 638]. In so doing, he sounded the real death knell of the 'Workers' and Peasants' Power'. Later that year between 14 and 16 July, Kohl and Genscher visited the Soviet Union again. This time Gorbachev consented to Germany's membership of NATO – a monumental concession [69: 639]. The distinguished historian of the Cold War, John Gaddis, is surely right when he says that there had never been a more deserving winner of the Nobel Peace Prize [66: 257]. This is not a view shared by all historians. Arvid Nelson, for example, downplays the contribution of Gorbachev, claiming that his 'commitment to reform was no stronger than his influence on his client states' leaders' [158: 179]. Instead, he argues, a 'combination of economic and ecological decline and increased popular awareness' condemned the country 'to oblivion' [158: 142]. Jonathan Grix contends that scholars have overemphasized the external factors in the GDR's collapse [85: 2].

The disintegration of the Soviet bloc is best characterized as a revolution wrapped up in decolonization [145: 157]. Never before had an empire melted away so quickly and so peacefully. The KGB accepted its implosion with much less grace than Gorbachev. It even 'devised active measures' to preserve the East European Communist regimes 'but was refused permission to implement them' [5: 706]. A heated debate raged inside the CPSU about the dramatic developments taking place in the region. Egor Ligachev, for example, abhorred the implosion of the Communist Parties and the concomitant loss of Soviet influence. Hardliners like V. Zhurkin, Director of the Institute of Europe at the USSR Academy of Sciences, charged the Kremlin with forsaking the 'Socialist community' and sacrificing Eastern Europe to capitalism. As for the Soviet military, they were deeply perturbed by events and believed their country's security interests were being violated [75: 165]. The Soviet Foreign Minister, Eduard Shevardnadze, was castigated in his own country for the loss of the GDR and resigned in December 1990 [45: 158]. Zatlin's assertion that ordinary GDR citizens 'made unification inevitable by deploying the threat of continued migration and demanding integration with the FRG in continued demonstrations' [230: 338] overstates their influence and neglects the Soviet context.

The East German ship of state capsized in the tide of history, leaving Gorbachev with a choice: surf the wave or close the floodgates. He chose the former and Germany was reunited as a Capitalist democracy at the heart of the European Community and NATO [145: 170]. Why did Gorbachev sanction the GDR's demise, something that had been unthinkable only a few months previously? Given that there were up to 400,000 Soviet troops stationed there, its dissolution could certainly have been prevented. There are three reasons for his momentous decision. First, the Soviet Union was in desperate need of financial assistance. Without it, his economic reforms could not succeed. As the European Community's wealthiest member, West Germany was in a position to help [145: 170]. Secondly, a 'Tiananmen Square' solution in the GDR would have seriously damaged Gorbachev's credibility as an international statesman, jeopardizing his new relationship with the West and refreezing the Cold War he had worked so hard to thaw. Thirdly, Gorbachev could hardly disregard the wishes of most East Germans after stating that all countries were free to choose their own destinies [45: 158].

The decisive contribution of Gorbachev does not detract from the colossal courage shown by ordinary citizens who took to the streets in their hundreds of thousands to topple the Communist system. It was their popular pressure in the face of an uncertain regime response that forced the SED to concede power. Without the 'wave of history' they generated, the GDR would not have been swept away [145: 171]. As Maier correctly observes, 'at each critical juncture, the East Germans' collective action – no matter how hesitant at first, and how filled with doubts later – impelled decisive accommodations or allowed new initiatives' [133: xiv]. In the end, however, they had Gorbachev to thank for their success, and for this reason he must take most credit for the collapse of the 'first "Workers' and Peasants' State" on German soil'. Seldom before in history had so much been owed by so many to one man [145: 171]. Until the mid-1980s, the people of this state had been told that 'to learn from the Soviet Union is to learn how to win'. With the advent of Gorbachev's reforms in the USSR, they were able to turn this slogan against their political masters [71: 65]. The GDR's dependence on the Soviet Union was ultimately its undoing [145: 171]. In his book on the 1989 Revolution in East Germany, Ilko-Sascha Kowalczuk states that 'history is not made by great men' [117: 34]. Yet Gorbachev shows that 'great men' can and sometimes do make history, even if, like everyone else, they are subject to the law of unintended consequences.

The role of Western leaders

Western leaders accepted a united Germany once it became clear that the GDR was doomed. America's 41st President, George H. W. Bush, strongly advocated Germany's reunification as a democratic, Capitalist country within NATO. After initial opposition, the French President, Francois Mitterand, came on side in return for a promise that the enlarged FRG would support a single European currency. Despite the best efforts of the British Prime Minister, Margaret Thatcher, a genuinely democratic East Germany could not have survived as a separate state in 1990. Documents released by the British Foreign and Commonwealth Office on 11 September 2009 reveal the depth of Thatcher and Mitterand's anxiety about German reunification in the first two months after the fall of the Berlin Wall [192]. However, their frantic efforts to persuade Gorbachev to block the process came to nothing.

Helmut Kohl became Germany's second 'unity Chancellor' by heeding the advice of the first, Otto von Bismarck: 'During its great events, the train of world history does not travel at a constant speed. No, it moves forward jerkily but then with irresistible power. All one can do is listen for the steps of God running through events, then jump and catch hold of His coattails as He rushes past' [9: 27]. On 28 November 1989, Kohl seized the initiative with a 'ten-point programme' to heal the division of Germany and Europe [69: 636]. But as the train of world history accelerated, his timetable became out of date. Kohl's achievement was to keep revising it so as to be first on the platform when the train arrived. That said, it was Gorbachev more than anyone else who ensured there were no derailments.

The role of the Stasi

According to one study, the Stasi's 'failure to perceive the deep-rootedness of discontent with the Socialist state throughout society' played a key role in the GDR's demise [28: 192]. In typical totalitarian fashion, its central analytical department made recommendations which prioritized ideology over 'tactical reforms' [28: 183]. On 31 August 1989, Mielke discussed the domestic situation with representatives of the MfS provincial administrations. In an allusion to the 1953 uprising, Mielke asked the representative from Gera: 'Has the day before 17 June arrived?' The reply he received was reassuring: 'It hasn't, and it won't arrive, that's what we're here for' [28: 186].

The ministry also found it difficult to read the intentions of the Kremlin because it did not spy on the USSR [76: 379–80]. Mielke had his hands full waging the class struggle at home and in the West. To open a third front against the Mecca of communism was, in any case, unthinkable. On 21 October 1989, three days after the overthrow of Honecker, Mielke warned his MfS top brass that the GDR could not distance itself from the Soviet Union [152: 500]. Yet as Childs and Popplewell rightly point out: '*Perestroika* was the ideological threat which proved fatal to the SED' [28: 184].

That the Stasi ultimately refrained from crushing the East German Revolution corroborates Koehler's argument that it was not 'a state within a state'. It was beholden to the party. The leash constraining the secret police might have been a long one but it was tight enough to ensure that the Rottweiler did not attack its owner [112: 30]. The large number of Stasi informers involved in the revolution spawned the misconception that the *Wende* was the result of an MfS conspiracy [152: 533]. The ministry persistently attempted to contain the opposition until the start of October 1989 [171: 268]. Although Mielke helped Krenz to remove Honecker, he remained a defender of the system until the last [171: 267]. The considerable influence exercised by IMs within the opposition movement was due to the ministry's success in infiltrating it. In order to demonstrate their *bona fides* to the dissidents, IMs ended up inadvertently radicalizing the revolution [152: 532]. With the *Wende* in full spate, some Stasi informants then emerged, genuinely or otherwise, as opponents of the system. As Peterson argues, there were some in the MfS who really did favour reform [171: 268].

The debt crisis

Apparently, East Germany had run up a foreign deficit of US$26.5 billion by the end of October 1989 [133: 59]. But as Garton Ash has pointed out, states do not just go bust, like businesses. Rather they default on their debts, as South American nations have done [71: 161]. Hungary and Poland were also mired in debt, yet were not erased from the map of Europe. Most SED leaders had no idea about the GDR's parlous finances, so could not have been demoralized by them. Instead, they believed their own mendacious propaganda [71: 161]. Incredibly, at the end of 1989 and after Honecker's overthrow, the Economics Minister, Christa Luft, still did not know the true extent of East Germany's indebtedness to foreign countries [56: 17]. Besides, on the eve of the revolution, the Federal Republic showed every indication of being willing to continue subsidizing the 'Workers' and Peasants' Power' [71: 161]. The debt crisis is significant in that it helped convince Gorbachev that the GDR was not worth defending. After all, the USSR lacked the financial resources to bail her out.

Protestant Revolution?

The role of the churches in bringing down the SED regime [24; 57] has persuaded some that what occurred in East Germany was a 'Protestant Revolution' [181; 160: 21–9]. While there is a degree of truth in this interpretation, it is an exaggeration.

As Burleigh points out, the GDR was the only Communist country with a Protestant majority [25: 436]. Its churches constituted one of the few public venues where opposition activists could congregate 'because any other gatherings of more than half a dozen people required the state's permission' [25: 444]. In May 1989, they provided sanctuary to groups observing the conduct of the fraudulent local elections [25: 447]. The following month the Stasi calculated that 'there were 2,500 hardcore opponents of the regime who met in as many as 160 groups. All but ten of these (the chief exception being the Initiative for Peace and Human

Rights) met under the aegis of the churches' [25: 445]. During
the GDR's 40th anniversary celebrations, 'the Evangelical Church
organized prayers for peace and vigils in Berlin, Leipzig and
Dresden, which were attended by hundreds of thousands of people' [25: 447]. The country's first free election in March 1990 produced a *Volkskammer* containing 14 Protestant pastors [25: 448].
There were also five pastors in the new administration headed by
Christian Democrat Lothar de Maizière [39: 281]. One of its first
initiatives was to reinstate Christian holy days [25: 448].

On the other hand, it is important to remember that membership of the East German Churches had fallen precipitously during
the Communist years. While secularization affected most European
countries, 40 years of SED totalitarianism had produced the least
devout society in the Soviet bloc, 'with only about ten per cent of
the GDR population acknowledging any religious affiliation' [25:
436]. Many opposition groups in the country used the churches for
their own purposes, while eschewing Christianity. As for ministers
of religion and theologians, they could not always be relied upon
to provide refuge [133: 173]. Some played ambiguous roles, afford-
ing a measure of protection, on the one hand, and limiting dissident activity, on the other. A number even became Stasi informants.
Many East Germans who participated in the *Wende* did so independ-
ently of the churches. Surveys in Leipzig show that church members
took part 'only slightly more frequently than non-members in general protests and that no difference existed as regards participation
in demonstrations' [39: 281]. The term 'Protestant Revolution' also
excludes the one million Roman Catholics living in the GDR.

Class revolution or revolution of 'rising expectations'?

According to Konrad Jarausch, the *Wende* was not a class revolution but a revolution of 'rising expectations' [99: 50–1]. In reality,
it was both. The party and state bureaucracy formed a socio-political class parasitical on the rest of society. Its privileges were particularly offensive because they so blatantly contradicted the Socialist
language of equality. From 1960 until 1989, SED leaders inhabited
a closely guarded forest community in the suburbs of East Berlin
called Wandlitz, which further isolated them from the very workers
and peasants they claimed to represent. Their living quarters were

far superior to those of ordinary East Germans [26: 1–2]. So-called Intershops, full of Western products, catered for their every need, while the majority of the population had to make do with systemic shortages and inferior goods from the Soviet bloc. SED hunting lodges were almost feudal in character, making a mockery of any Communist pretensions. Party leaders 'secretly drank wine and publicly preached water', to use the words of the famous nineteenth-century German poet, Heinrich Heine. In 1989–90, this ruling class was overthrown in a revolution representing nearly all sections of East German society.

Honecker had once admonished his comrades that 'the people need cheap bread, a dry flat, and a job. If these three things are in order, socialism is secure' [36: 134]. By the 1980s, however, most GDR citizens wanted and expected more. The younger generation in particular craved Western life-styles and better career prospects. Above all, they demanded the right to travel freely. As Anna Saunders has argued, the SED's attempts to impose patriotism on them from above were unsuccessful [194: 232]. While living standards in the Bonn Republic rose relentlessly, those in the 'workers' and peasants' paradise' stagnated. East Germans did not compare themselves to their Czech, Polish, or Hungarian neighbours but to their cousins in the Federal Republic. With the exception of the north-eastern corner of Pomerania and 'the valley of the clueless' around Dresden, West German television could be watched across the GDR [210: 29]. As a result, its inhabitants were all too aware of their relative backwardness. Although Dale points out that 'numerous cases can be found in which rising expectations do not lead to revolutionary situations' [36: 226], the GDR's status as a Cold War state abutting West Germany had a great impact on the expectations of its populace.

'*Wende* in the *Wende*'

The philosopher, Jürgen Habermas, has conceptualized the events of 1989–90 in East Germany as a 'catch-up revolution' [86]. He ignores the fact that its initiators favoured a more direct, grass-roots democracy than that pertaining in Bonn [190: 145]. They also wanted to reform the GDR, not liquidate it. However, they were soon swept aside by the majority of East Germans, who demanded reunification with the Capitalist, democratic Federal Republic. This amounted to what Meuschel calls a '*Wende* in the *Wende*' [151: 316, 318].

East Germans voted communism out of existence on 18 March 1990 in their first free elections since 1932. With the victory of the centre-right's 'Alliance for Germany', the 'Workers' and Peasants' Power' lost its inner purpose. To quote Ulrich Beck, 'Poland minus communism is still Poland; but the German Democratic Republic minus communism is – the Federal Republic' [190: 92]. By now the *Deutschmark* had become emblematic of most East Germans' desire for unity: 'If you don't come to us, we will go to you', they chanted [117: 463]. On 1 July, German economic, monetary, and social union came into force. Three months later, on 3 October 1990, the GDR joined the Federal Republic of Germany under Article 23 of its Basic Law. Any doubt about the support of easterners was dispelled on 2 December that year, when Kohl's Conservative–Liberal coalition won a majority of 134 in the first all-German elections to the federal parliament [69: 640].

That the revolutionaries of the first hour failed to prevent the GDR's collapse into the arms of the Federal Republic has been attributed by Meuschel to the fact that East Germany was a 'classless society'. In this respect, she claims, it differed from Poland and Hungary, which had already produced alternative elites capable of steering their respective revolutions to successful conclusions [151: 319–20]. Regardless of class, the end result of all the revolutions across Eastern Europe was the same: the restoration of capitalism. The main reasons for the '*Wende* in the *Wende*' were the GDR's lack of popular legitimacy and the magnetic pull of the Federal Republic. A secondary factor was the success of SED totalitarianism in isolating the various opposition groups during the 1980s.

This was the first essentially peaceful and successful revolution in the history of Germany [59: 3]. What began as a movement against totalitarianism in the GDR quickly became a movement for liberal democracy, capitalism and national unity. For the first time on German soil all three triumphed simultaneously. Far from derailing the revolution, the '*Wende* in the *Wende*' consummated it. As a result, the dreams of 1848 were finally realized. The dissolution of the GDR along with its social system made the year 1990 more decisive in some ways than 1918 or 1933 [219: 191]. After the fall of the Iron Curtain, the perennial 'German question' was finally solved. Germany's reunification must surely rank as one of the most serendipitous events of the twentieth century.

Conclusion: Obituary

'Ostalgie'

The adage 'the past is a foreign country'* seems particularly apt for the 40-year-old GDR, which can now only be visited in the history books. More than two decades after East Germany vanished from the atlas, the expanded Federal Republic is still grappling with its legacy. Almost totally discredited in 1990, the GDR has undergone something of a popular rehabilitation since then, at least among its former inhabitants. The neologism *'Ostalgie'* ('nostalgia for the East') was coined to describe this phenomenon. According to one survey in 2009, more than half of east Germans thought the GDR 'was not a bad country'. Forty-nine per cent agreed that it had 'more good sides than bad'; a further eight per cent thought 'that people lived better and more happily in the GDR than today' [216]. Many miss the country's welfare provisions. But there is also affection for its material culture [191: 226]. While nostalgia for the Third Reich faded as the West German economy boomed, memories of the GDR have followed the opposite trajectory.

There are several reasons for this. An idealized view of the 'golden West', a product of four decades behind the Iron Curtain, quickly came up against prosaic reality. The 'blooming landscapes' promised by Chancellor Kohl failed to bloom in many parts of eastern Germany after reunification. Retrospective pining for the social protection afforded by the SED regime was rendered all the more poignant by the contemporary scourge of unemployment, something that had not been experienced since the early 1930s. More than a few Westerners displayed contempt for the experiences of those who had lived under state socialism. The sudden, wholesale adoption of the West German model caused some easterners to feel disorientated, disempowered, or even 'colonized' in

112

the enlarged Federal Republic [31: 1–26]. Willy Brandt's famous prediction, made after the fall of the Berlin Wall, that 'now everything [would] grow together that belong[ed] together' [31: vii] seemed to be happening too slowly or not at all. When the natural catharsis that accompanied the GDR's demise subsided, many came to believe that to condemn their former country out of hand was somehow to condemn their own lives within it. Since the crimes of the East German dictatorship pale in comparison to those of the Third Reich, they were more easily marginalized within the collective memory. To quote Margherita von Brentano: 'The Third Reich left behind mountains of corpses. The GDR left behind mountains of catalogue cards' [190: 159].

Certainly *'Ostalgie'* is 'not what it used to be'. Even so, it cannot simply be dismissed as an exercise in whitewashing. Most 'ostalgic' Germans do not deny the darker sides of the SED dictatorship; they just underplay them. Neither do they hanker after a lost 'workers' and peasants' paradise'. For all their concerns, most still prefer the FRG to the GDR. In the final analysis, the history of the GDR was not one of black and white but of black and grey; not one of negatives and positives, but one of negatives and partial positives. During the first decade of the twenty-first century, scholars found it easier to transcend the condemnatory-exculpatory discourse that dominated the debate about East Germany in the 1990s [134: 280–4].

Negatives

The negatives of the GDR are clear and largely uncontested: a metastasizing Stasi; the absence of genuine democracy; the legitimacy deficit; certain human rights abuses; the use of torture in jails; restrictions on travel to Capitalist countries; the shooting of refugees attempting to flee the republic; the state kidnapping of children whose parents were intent on decamping to the West; misleading propaganda; corruption among party and state officials; shortages of certain goods in the shops; a lack of choice with regard to just about everything; increasing militarization; regimentation of the population; and severe environmental degradation.

Allinson claims that between 1949 and 1990 the GDR 'had as much (or as little) right to exist as the FRG' [2: 8]. Yet while the

Federal Republic underwent a process of internal legitimization through free-and-fair elections, those in the GDR were rigged as a matter of course. East German support for the 'Workers' and Peasants' State' never exceeded 30 per cent and usually fell well below that, according to Valentin Falin, the Soviet diplomat and German specialist [26: 32]. It is therefore difficult to disagree with the assessment of Eric Hobsbawm that 'the East German regime suffered from the patent fact that it had no legitimacy, initially almost no support, and would have never in its lifetime won a freely contested election' [96: 148–9].

According to Kettenacker, 'in 50 or 100 years' time' it is probable that the SED state 'will be remembered as ... the "Stasi State"' [107: 238]. Helmut Müller-Enbergs estimates that over the course of the GDR's history, approximately 250,000 full-time employees and 600,000 informers worked for the MfS [40: 90]. In a groundbreaking study, Bruce has shed light on its sophisticated operations at local level [23]. Yet, as Bruce himself reminds us, while the ministry was the party's principal instrument for controlling society, other organizations were also involved. These included the official trade union (FDGB), the Communist youth movement (FDJ), SED factory cells (GO), the People's Police and their collaborators, teachers, neighbourhood governing associations, printed media, and the 'Agitation Commission' of the SED [23: 184]. The fact that the GDR was a fanatical surveillance society is becoming ever less remarkable, given the proliferation of surveillance in Western countries.

While East Germany certainly lacked the fundamentals of a *Rechtsstaat* or 'state under the rule of law', to label the country an *Unrechtsstaat* or 'unjust state' [40: 62] is going too far because it implies that no justice at all was dispensed on its territory. How 'Socialist law' was experienced by ordinary East Germans is the subject of a recent study by Inga Markovits [139].

Socio-cultural achievements

The GDR's socio-cultural achievements have been evaluated by Bollinger and Vilmar [16]. Certainly many welfare services became 'extensive' in the 'Workers' and Peasants' Power' [197: 214]. Officially, there was full employment. Infant mortality was low and life expectancy was approximately the same as in the Bonn Republic [169: 18]. Homelessness was not a problem. Rents and prices were subsidized, as were holidays. The cost of a tram ticket in the 1980s was no higher than at the end of the Second World War [134: 11]. Bread queues were a thing of the past and basic foodstuffs were inexpensive. In 1989, meat consumption, traditionally the primary indicator of well-being, was equal to that of the FRG [197: 214]. Levels of drug abuse, pornography, prostitution and street crime were also said to bc lower than in the West. It would not be inaccurate to claim that the social rights enshrined in the United Nations' 1948 Universal Declaration of Human Rights were more fully realized in East Germany than in some Capitalist countries.

Yet care and repression were not always separable in the GDR. Hospitals, for example, were 'heavily penetrated' by the Stasi [23: 160]. The 'right to work' was constitutionally protected but those who challenged political orthodoxy could be debarred from practising their profession [110]. Furthermore, the GDR's welfare state was a nanny state *par excellence*. Individual initiative was stymied because East Germans were conditioned to regard their benefits as entitlements rather than rewards. As Zatlin points out, the SED failed to 'develop a participatory procedure that might have made East Germans feel responsible for the services they used' [230: 54].

Government propaganda gave a varnished and occasionally mendacious account of social accomplishments. Although nobody faced destitution as a consequence of personal misfortune, the extent of welfare provision was sometimes rather limited, particularly in the case of pensions. This persuaded many to continue working, thereby easing labour shortages. Many hospitals were badly equipped by contemporary standards, even if the outpatient polyclinics provided an adequate service [169: 17–18]. Full employment did not necessarily mean that people were gainfully employed [169: 17]. Often it meant doing the job that the state told you to do. On 12 October 1988, 'the three millionth flat' built since 1971 was handed over [220: 341], yet there was still a lack of housing. Moreover, Honecker's housing estates were built at the expense of old town centres, which fell into disrepair.♦ It would be unsurprising if levels of street crime were somewhat lower in the GDR than in West Germany, because the former was a police state. The fact that crime was so seldom reported by the East German media helped foster the impression that this was a 'relatively crime-free' republic [26: 31].

Ultimately, over 90 per cent of women were in paid employment, compared to less than 50 per cent in the Federal Republic [219: 193]. However, they usually had to contend with doing most of the household chores as well [17: 79]. Educational opportunities were equal for children of both sexes after the 1960s [222: 376]. Still, the education system both undermined and reinforced traditional notions of gender [49: 54–68]. Most of the leading positions in society were occupied by men. Harsch is right to argue that the party's domination of political debate and its repression of 'civil society' prevented the emergence of 'an independent women's movement that might have developed a fundamental critique of the gendered foundations of SED ideology, popular attitudes, spousal relations and economic structures' [134: 167]. Among 'the most salient values of the regime', according to Epstein, was 'a pronounced masculinity' [47: 262]. Ansorg and Hürtgen have gone so far as to claim that 'female emancipation' in the GDR was a 'myth' [98: 163–76]. More persuasive is Weitz's contention that 'by the 1980s, "real existing socialism" had produced all the emancipation of which it was capable' [222: 380].

As Stuart Parkes has pointed out, 'In the GDR, it was largely impossible to sink; it was equally impossible for the overwhelming majority to rise, whatever their talents, beyond a modest level of comfort' [169: 21]. A corollary to this was that the pace of life was slower than in the West. Some GDR citizens, particularly in retrospect, regarded this as something to be cherished, a rejection of the Capitalist 'rat race' or the so-called *Ellbogengesellschaft* (literally 'elbow society', or society where the weakest go to the wall). Productivity in the workplace might have been lower but so were stress levels [169: 15]. Of course, a slower pace of life could also mean a more frustrating one, particularly when dealing with the bureaucracy or shopping for scarce commodities.

Andrew Port has exploded the myth of a mutually supportive *Schicksalsgemeinschaft* ('community of fate') or *Notgemeinschaft* ('community born of necessity') during the Ulbricht years [174: 276–77]. The notion became even more fanciful as the Stasi drilled down deeper into society during the 1970s and 1980s. A particularly shocking case is that of the opposition activist, Vera Wollenberger, who discovered after the *Wende* that her own husband, Knud, had been informing on her for years [169: 21; 70: 18]. 'IM Donald', to use his MfS alias, had been more than a Red under the bed; he had been a Red *in* the bed! The couple are now divorced. In reality, of course, the Stasi was neither omnipresent nor omniscient. But many East Germans believed that it was and behaved accordingly [24: 106].

If such a *Schicksalsgemeinschaft* really existed, one wonders why the GDR had one of the highest suicide rates in the world [80: 27]. In general, Udo Grashoff argues, this was not due to the SED dictatorship. Key variables, according to him, were the area's traditions and Protestant heritage [80: 120–1]. Thuringia and Saxony had displayed high suicide rates since the mid-nineteenth century [80: 48]. For cultural and religious reasons, Protestant regions tend to record higher suicide rates than Catholic ones [80: 50]. The question then arises as to why other Protestant countries fared better. Certainly the SED regime failed to improve the situation. It wanted to avoid the negative publicity of high suicide statistics because they seemed to indicate that all was not well with East German society. When the figures rose in 1963 and 1977, the Politburo prohibited their dissemination [80: 470].

The standard of education in the 'Workers' and Peasants' State' was generally high and the SED widened access to workers' and farmers' children. Yet schools were also sites of authoritarianism and indoctrination [130: 66; 26: 33]. A place at a higher education institution could be denied for political reasons. Young males 'stood little chance of entering university at all unless they had volunteered for three years' military service rather than the basic 18 months' [169: 18]. As John Connelly has demonstrated, East German universities were more thoroughly Sovietized between 1945 and 1956 than their Polish or Czech counterparts [29]. Moreover, by the late 1960s the bourgeois academic elite had been replaced by a loyal Socialist intelligentsia [101]. The lack of student participation in the 1989 Revolution can be attributed to three factors: the Stasi's infestation of universities, the fact that only politically reliable youngsters could gain admission, and the new educational opportunities created by the regime.

While East Germany boasted some famous cultural figures (for example, the dramatist, producer and poet, Bertolt Brecht; the writers Christa Wolf and Stefan Heym), it stifled creativity with its oxymoronic doctrine of 'Socialist realism'. On the one hand, the SED facilitated worthy cultural activities and ensured that more people than ever before had access to them. On the other, it persecuted its critics (even if they were Communists) and sought to control all aspects of cultural life. Some intellectuals joined the refugee exodus during the 1950s. Periods of greater official tolerance under Ulbricht (1963–5) and Honecker (1971–6) were dramatically curtailed. The Stasi thoroughly penetrated the artistic and intellectual community, including the 'alternative' Prenzlauer Berg scene in East Berlin during the 1980s [195: 79–108]. Still, it was possible for writers and poets to push back the boundaries of official cultural discourse, as studies by Karen Leeder and Helen Bridge have shown [120; 19].

Sporting achievements

State provision focussed solely on the Olympic sports [18: 428]. Although the GDR won many Olympic gold medals, some of them were the result of the Stasi's criminal drugs programme. From 1969 to November 1989 'more than 10,000 East German athletes were doped' and only one was officially caught [153: 141–2]. Unfortunately, these drugs sometimes had harmful side effects, as illustrated by the case of Heidi Krieger, who won gold for shot-put at the 1986 European Championships in Stuttgart. After being fed a massive dose of anabolic steroids, she began turning into a man. The emotional problems she suffered as a transsexual caused her to have a sex-change operation in 1997. She is now Andreas Krieger [153: 137–46]. Sports regarded as 'politically unnecessary' were either proscribed or allowed to atrophy [18: 428].

Anti-fascism

Anti-fascism was the foundation myth of the 'Workers' and Peasants' State'. German opposition to National Socialism is best encapsulated in the phrase 'resistance without the people', giving the lie to Communist claims that they led a united and successful resistance between 1933 and 1945. Yet according to Judt 'long after 1989 children in eastern German secondary schools continued to believe that east German troops had fought alongside the Red Army to liberate their country from Hitler' [103: 642]. Although individual Communists suffered terribly at the hands of the Nazis, and many fought bravely against them, theirs was often a tale of defeat and failure rather than glory and success. In the early 1930s, the KPD had regarded Social Democracy, not National Socialism, as the main enemy. With the signing of the Molotov-Ribbentrop Pact in August 1939, the Communists had stopped resisting the Nazis altogether – a situation that changed only when Hitler invaded the Soviet Union in June 1941.

With the formation of the GDR, the SED hijacked anti-fascism to provide ideological justification for its totalitarian dictatorship. Already in June 1945, Ulbricht had disbanded the anti-fascist committees that had sprung up spontaneously in the aftermath of the Second World War [123: 469–79]. For party leaders, the 1933 definition of fascism devised by the head of the Comintern, Georgi Dimitrov, was still valid. According to him, fascism represented 'the open dictatorship of the most reactionary, most chauvinist and most imperialist elements of finance capital, which directs itself against the interests of the whole nation' [149: 73]. In other words, the GDR was anti-fascist only because it was Socialist. By blaming everything on the now dispossessed monopoly Capitalists and Junkers who had allegedly spawned National Socialism, the workers and peasants could be absolved of all responsibility for its crimes. Even better, they could retrospectively be declared 'victors over fascism'. The re-emergence of neo-Nazi activity in the GDR during the 1970s and 1980s was, in part, a reaction to the relentless anti-fascism of the SED – a kind of 'anti-anti-fascism'. For the party, however, it was a product of 'West German influences and individual asocial behaviour' [163: 141].

The Nazi persecution and genocide of the Jews was hardly discussed in the GDR. Israel came to be perceived by the SED as an 'imperialist' power similar in its expansionist aims to the Third Reich [212: 83]. While the Federal Republic paid compensation to the Jewish state, the GDR refused to follow suit [212: 80, 83]. Although anti-Zionism and anti-Semitism are discrete phenomena, the former did build upon the latter in the GDR [214]. In early September 1968, the Nazi-hunter, Simon Wiesenthal, released a study entitled 'The same language: first for Hitler – now for Ulbricht', which dealt with the Arab–Israeli War of June 1967. Wiesenthal noticed that some passages in the GDR press bore a striking resemblance to comments made in the Nazi media. It subsequently transpired that the anti-Israeli articles had been penned by the very same people who, during the National Socialist era, had written pieces denouncing the 'Jewish threat'. Wiesenthal believed 'that there were even groups of Nazis among the editorial staff of newspapers like *Neues Deutschland* and *Deutsche Außenpolitik*' [20: 212–13]. Notwithstanding the pro-Arab stance of the Soviet bloc, GDR coverage of the 1967 Six-Day War had been particularly biased against Israel [20: 212–13].

Still, some progress was made on the Jewish issue as a consequence of *Ostpolitik*. In the end, however, the 1989–90 Revolution ensured that the SED never had to reverse its position of 'non-responsibility' [212: 84]. By largely ignoring the racial dimension, the party was denying Nazism's *raison d'être*. The first declaration of the freely elected East German parliament in March 1990 apologized for the Holocaust and took historical responsibility for the crimes of National Socialism. Furthermore, it asked 'the people of Israel for forgiveness for the hypocrisy and hostility of official GDR policy towards the state of Israel and for the persecution and degradation of Jewish fellow-citizens in our country since 1945' [26: 137].

The GDR failed to acknowledge other victims of the Third Reich, such as gypsies, homosexuals, the hereditarily ill, and 'asocials'. Worse still, it continued Nazism's persecution of the Jehovah's Witnesses [38]. The Nazis had also denied the discrete ethnic identity of the Sorbs, banning their Slavonic language and customs from the public realm [11: 20]. According to Peter Barker, the 'nationalities policy in the GDR was in its practice merely a variant on the policies of successive German administrations, namely one which accepted that continued assimilation was both inevitable and ultimately desirable. The difference was that the rhetoric of the policy claimed that it was aiming to preserve Sorbian culture' [11: 202]. Needless to say, the country's enthusiastic commemoration of Hitler's Communist opponents was at the expense of those from other political parties.

That said, like other legitimizing myths, East German anti-fascism did contain a kernel of truth. The party at least taught its population that fascism was 'evil' [20: 209]. It also paid generous pensions to those it designated 'anti-fascist resistance fighters', even if Jews persecuted solely on grounds of race were treated as second-class victims. Moreover, it provided sanctuary for almost 2,000 Marxist refugees from Pinochet's right-wing military dictatorship in Chile between 1973 and 1989 [141: 1]. By way of gratitude, Pinochet's democratic successors permitted Honecker to shelter in their Moscow embassy in 1992 and to spend the last months of his life on Chilean soil. Closer to home, East Germany opposed the quasi-fascist regimes of Franco in Spain and Salazar in Portugal.

Most importantly, the GDR authorities seem to have purged or prosecuted more Nazis than their West German counterparts, although East German efforts in this regard were much less impressive than contemporaries believed. For example, ex-Nazi teachers who had been thrown out of the door sometimes came back in through the windows. In Saxony approximately 25 per cent of those sacked had been given their jobs back by 1951 [60: 54]. As Judt points out, 'by the early 1950s, more than half the rectors of East German institutes of higher education were former Nazi Party members, as were over ten per cent of the parliament a decade later' [103: 60]. The Stasi and Gestapo were strikingly similar in certain respects, the former taking over 'many thousands' of the latter's functionaries and informants [103: 60]. According to an internal SED analysis in 1954, former National Socialists accounted for 25.4 per cent of the party's membership. In local, factory and district leaderships they often constituted the majority [84: 42, n136]. Of course, it should be noted that a significant degree of collaboration between the SED and former members of the NSDAP was inevitable, given the extent to which the German population had been mired in Nazism. If the SED had refused to work with all those who had been National Socialists, the economy and society of East Germany would simply have imploded.

The anti-fascist myth proved useful in maintaining the GDR's internal stability and burnishing its credentials as a 'respectable' member of the international community. Meuschel has elucidated how it simultaneously guaranteed the loyalty of an educated anti-fascist intelligentsia and suppressed any potential debate about 'Stalinism', thereby underpinning East Germany's reputation as one of the most stable countries in the Soviet bloc [151: 39–40]. In 1989 Christa Wolf conceded: 'We felt a strong inhibition about engaging in resistance against people who spent the Nazi period in concentration camps' [190: 169]. Many East Germans were anti-fascists without necessarily subscribing to the narrow definition of fascism enforced by the SED. Perhaps this is best illustrated by their 'multiple interpretations' of the Spanish Civil War – a defining experience for those German Communists who had fought against Franco during the 1930s [149: 202].

Once the Federal Republic began to address its National Socialist past from the late 1960s onwards, East Germany found it increasingly difficult to claim the moral high ground on this issue. Ultimately, the anti-fascist myth suffered from a 'fatal flaw': its credibility depended on the presence in government of those who had actually resisted the Nazis, or at least been persecuted by them. That the GDR unravelled immediately after the overthrow of Honecker in October 1989 is probably no coincidence. In the end, as Nothnagle observes, 'the anti-fascist covenant had been dissolved by the passing of the anti-fascist generation' [163: 141–2].

Foreign policy

'The right to live in peace', according to the SED, was 'the most important of all human rights' [8: 32]. However, the party's incessant propaganda depicting the 'Workers' and Peasants' State' as a 'bastion of peace' was one-sided. Not only did the GDR support the Soviet Army's crushing of the Hungarian Revolution in 1956, it was also implicated in the Warsaw Pact occupation of Czechoslovakia 12 years later. In 1979 it endorsed the Soviet invasion of Afghanistan [144: 193] and the following year Honecker advocated a similar solution to deal with the Solidarity trade union in Poland [224: 335–40].

On the other hand, the SED accepted the loss of East Prussia, recognizing the Oder–Neisse border with Poland in the 'Görlitz Agreement' of 6 July 1950 [69: 613]. The FRG, by way of contrast, continued to demand Germany's reunification within the borders of 1937 for another two decades. Moreover, the GDR did not attack West Berlin or the Federal Republic, even if it sought to undermine them. Despite the militarization of East German society, the SED was generally concerned to avoid military conflict with states on the other side of the Iron Curtain. After 1956 it pursued 'peaceful coexistence' and during the 1970s it embraced *détente*. Both too much and too little tension threatened the regime's stability, so it tried to maintain a semi-frozen peace based on the status quo. East Germany can hardly be accused of having pursued an unpredictable foreign policy. By helping to maintain the delicate balance of power between NATO and the Warsaw Pact on the front line, it reduced the likelihood of a hot war breaking out. Unlike the Third Reich, the GDR was not a warfare state. Even so, peace in the full sense of the word broke out only when the 'Workers' and Peasants' State' melted away with the Cold War snows. As Smyser has written, this conflict may not have started over Germany but it did come to centre on it [198: 71].

The GDR's foreign policy record in other respects is also mixed. On the negative side, it supported countless dictatorships. On 8 June 1989, it publicly defended the Tiananmen Square massacre in China [220: 343]. Peter-Michael Diestel, East Germany's Interior Minister from April to October 1990, would later comment that his country had become 'an Eldorado for terrorists' during the 1970s and 1980s [5: 389, 511; 28: 138]. Not only did the Stasi sponsor Arab groups dedicated to the destruction of Israel [112: 359–71]; it provided military training and safe havens for members of West Germany's Red Army Faction (RAF) [112: 387–401; 195: 142–62]. The ministry's insidious infiltration of the FRG and other states has been well documented [112: 149–264, 297–324; 76; 195: 109–41]. Its foreign intelligence service, the so-called Main Administration for Reconnaissance (*Hauptverwaltung Aufklärung*, or HVA) headed by Markus 'Mischa' Wolf, thoroughly penetrated the political, economic, and cultural life of the Bonn Republic [40: 195]. By his own admission, Wolf perfected 'the use of sex in spying', his stable of so-called Romeos (handsome young men who seduced lonely, vulnerable women into becoming spies) and Romiettes (attractive women who 'honey-trapped' men) proving very adept at ensnaring foreign targets [226: 135; 112: 177–87]. The Stasi recruited many West Germans by threatening to harm their relatives behind the Wall [112: 200]. It is often forgotten that, although the Soviet bloc lost the Cold War, it won the spying game with the West. The HVA, advantaged by being based in a closed and tightly controlled society but infiltrating an open and democratic one, played a crucial role in this victory.

On the positive side, the SED found itself in the unusual position of supporting a democratically elected President – Salvador Allende of Chile – after 1970. When Allende, a democratic Marxist, was overthrown in a US-backed military coup on 11 September 1973, the GDR severed diplomatic relations with Santiago [220: 319] and called for the return of constitutional government. The

SED's defence of the African National Congress (ANC) at a time when the United States government was still branding Nelson Mandela a 'terrorist' is also worth noting. Moreover, East Germany spoke up for the Palestinians in an era when most of the Western world barely acknowledged their existence. From 1955, the GDR provided political asylum to North Vietnamese Communists.

While dependence on the repressive and less-developed USSR brought numerous disadvantages for the GDR, there were also some advantages. Thousands of East Germans visited the Soviet Union as cultural ambassadors, tourists or exchange students, which helped to overcome the poisonous legacy of the Second World War. While many may have despised the Soviet leadership until 1985, they tended to get along better with ordinary Russians. There were countless examples of genuine friendships and happy marriages between people of both countries. These had the effect of lowering Soviet suspicions of Germany, paving the way for Gorbachev's decision to relinquish the GDR in 1990 [77b: 48–9]. But perhaps the greatest achievement of the 'Workers' and Peasants' Power' was the way it left the stage of history: not with a bang but with a whimper. In this sense, it could hardly have been more different from the Third Reich.

The 'normalization' thesis

In the view of the British historian, Mary Fulbrook, 'the GDR lasted … long enough for new generations to be socialised, to grow to maturity and to experience their everyday life as "perfectly normal"' [64: 8]. Mark Allinson avers 'that the GDR was quite a normal country' whose 'citizens for the most part led normal lives, dominated as in most countries by family life and concerns about work and material welfare' [2: 158]. Other 'Fulbrookians' have adopted similar positions [61; 131].

'Normality', of course, is a highly nebulous, subjective and relative term. Clearly there were things about the GDR that were anything but normal. A 'normal' country does not need to build a 155-kilometre wall to prevent a substantial part of its population from fleeing. Nor does it have to establish the most obsessive secret police in history and rely on approximately 400,000 Soviet troops to guarantee stability. It is as well to remember that to get by in this system one had to forgo the civil liberties enjoyed by citizens in the West. East Germans also had to accept, or at least not oppose, the dictatorship of the SED. The restrictions on travel to the FRG were felt particularly keenly by many, for obvious reasons. One has to wonder why such large numbers tried to leave if they experienced their lives as 'normal'.

That said, existence could seem 'normal' enough for others who were raised in the GDR and never experienced anything different [161b: 657]. After all, this was a relatively closed society subject to incessant propaganda, so its inhabitants were sometimes unaware of the injustices perpetrated by their government. The repressive aspects of the system, while remaining in the collective consciousness, retreated into the background so that people did not always feel like victims. Since the partial 'normalization' of abnormality was a significant victory for the SED, we need to draw a clear distinction between 'normality' and what became the 'norm' in East Germany. 'Routinization' [61: 13, 15, 68–75] is a better term to describe how significant numbers of East Germans became accustomed to the norms of life under state socialism. Such a thing really pertained only between 1961 and 1979, according to most 'Fulbrookians' [61].

Perceptions began to change as more citizens were granted permission to visit the Bonn Republic in the era of *Ostpolitik* [161b: 657]. For some, the epiphany did not come until the 1989 Revolution. As one East German later recounted, until her first trip to the FRG following the fall of the Berlin Wall, 'she had not realized the GDR was so grey, the buildings so decrepit, the air so dusty, because she had never known anything different' [59: 144]. Many who later described their lives in the 'Workers' and Peasants' State' as 'perfectly normal' appeared to have taken a different view in 1990. Their longer-term memories were tinged with '*Ostalgia*' and should therefore be treated with caution.

The 'normalization' thesis has been challenged by other historians too. In 2002, Clemens Vollnhals and Jürgen Weber edited a volume entitled *The Appearance of Normality*. According to them, everyday life in the GDR was 'always saturated' by the 'threats and potentially drastic interventions of the regime' [218]. Eli Rubin argues that 'East German society was not normal in any conceivable way but, rather, was a wholly unique confluence of bottom-up influences; external influences; economic conditions; pre-existing notions about aesthetics, gender, and material values; and the centralizing impulse of the GDR's command economy' [191: 8]. In an innovative study, Jan Palmowski rejects what he sees as the value-laden concept of 'normalization' because it 'obstructs, rather than creates, a more sophisticated understanding of how different spheres of power related to everyday life' [168: 311]. Instead, he proposes the notion of the 'public transcript', which 'simply asserts that in accepting the public transcript of socialism, most citizens accepted the party's power as unavoidable' [168: 312]. He argues that 'most East Germans never appropriated the GDR as "their" nation' [168: 20]. Rather they 'developed rival meanings of nationhood and identity' and 'learned to mask their growing distance from socialism beneath regular public assertions of Socialist belonging' [168: i]. While this helped to perpetuate the SED regime, it also made it very easy for citizens to renounce the GDR in 1989 [168: i].

Was the GDR doomed from the start?

The thesis that the history of the GDR was essentially a 'countdown at whose end could only be its downfall' is misjudged [152: 8]. Certainly East Germany began life with certain disadvantages. A relatively small state of fewer than 20 million people, it lacked raw materials and had to pay vast reparations to the Soviet Union. It was also cut off from its natural hinterlands in the West, occupied by a less-developed country, and subjected to economic warfare by the Federal Republic until 1961. After an illegitimate birth, the GDR suffered a traumatic childhood. It then suffered the repression of its teenage years before failing to overcome deep-seated problems during the 1970s. By 1989 the GDR was succumbing to an existential midlife crisis.

However, we must guard against 'the illusions of retrospective determinism', to use the words of the French philosopher, Henri Bergson [71: 161]. In the late 1940s, the East German Communists had been confident that history was on their side. This was not just a case of ideological self-delusion [201: 114–15]. Capitalism had crashed in the 1930s just when the USSR was experiencing rapid economic growth. The latter's economic system had stood the test of war and communism seemed to be on the march everywhere.

China became a 'People's Republic' in the same year that the GDR was founded.

When the Second World War broke out, 'industrial production per head in the region that would a decade later become the GDR amounted to 725 *Reichsmarks* per year. In the territories that would become West Germany, production per head was only 609 *Reichsmarks*' [211: 575]. Childs contends that: 'In 1945 the part of Germany which became the Soviet Zone and then the GDR was possibly the most modern area of Europe' [26: 22]. According to Nelson, Allied bombing had 'destroyed less than 12 per cent of Soviet Zone housing, but more than 25 per cent of western Germany's' [158: 31]. Aerial bombardment had 'cut western German industrial productivity by 21 per cent compared to a 15 per cent cut in eastern Germany. After the war the Soviet Zone was more than self-sufficient in food, whereas western Germany … depended on imports from the east' [158: 31]. In other words, the east started off with certain advantages over the west. It was far from clear in 1949 that the Bonn Republic would prove the more successful of the two German states. It had the after-effects of Allied bombing to contend with and the 'economic miracle' only really got underway in the mid-1950s. Neither was it a foregone conclusion that the self-destructive tendencies of capitalism would be tamed.

The argument that the GDR was predestined for the dustbin of history is also based on the unproven assumption that a similar fate awaited the Soviet empire. After all, the regime in East Berlin was guaranteed by the one in the Kremlin. In the view of Fulbrook, the end result was by no means inevitable [59: 282]. Yet as its economic system became increasingly antiquated, the probability of the GDR's failure grew with each passing year.

Why was the collapse of East Germany not predicted?

Hardly anybody, not even the most qualified political scientists, predicted the GDR's demise. This is because it appeared to be one of the most stable states in the Soviet bloc. The World Bank ranked it among the top ten leading industrialized countries, in the same league as Great Britain and Italy, despite the fact that its economy was probably weaker than those of Poland and Hungary [158: 183].

One of East Germany's most successful exports was spurious performance statistics [103: 611]. The fact that it was a relatively closed society also hampered Western efforts to assess the true situation. It is in the nature of totalitarian polities to present a facade of order and efficiency to the outside world.

Having said that, fault also lies with the Western observers themselves. In the era of *Ostpolitik*, most academics in the FRG moved away from swingeing critiques of the GDR to analyses of why it was proving so stable. As totalitarianism theory went out of fashion in the late 1960s, historians and political scientists tried to understand East Germany in its own terms (the so-called *Immanenzansatz*) rather than according to external criteria of evaluation. All too often they understated the repressive features of the regime and neglected its systemic failures. For example, the index of Jonathan Steele's *Socialism with a German Face* does not even mention the Stasi [207]. Few scholars wrote about the Ministry for State Security or resistance during these years. An honourable exception was Karl Wilhelm Fricke [51; 52]. The first book in English on the MfS did not appear until 1996 [28]. Historians more hostile to the GDR rightly emphasized its dependence on the USSR. Yet the Soviet Union seemed a permanent feature of the geopolitical landscape until the late 1980s.

Why did the GDR last so long?

In 1990 one of the GDR's most celebrated writers, Stefan Heym, predicted that his country would become a mere 'footnote in world history' [158: 188; 170: 3; 21: 799]. So far his fears have proved unfounded. In any case, the footnote would be rather an extensive one, since the 'first Workers' and Peasants' Power on German soil' lasted longer than the 14-year-old Weimar Republic and the 12-year-old Third Reich combined. Indeed, if one counts its prehistory between 1945 and 1949, the GDR was almost the same age as the post-1871 Second Empire when it died [219: 191].

What, then, accounts for its longevity? There are six reasons, listed here in descending order of importance. The first is repression and the threat of it. Not all historians agree that this was the principal factor [174: 69, 279], yet Soviet troops stationed in the country guaranteed its existence for 40 years. As Leonid Brezhnev told Erich Honecker on 28 July 1970: 'Without us, there would be no GDR'

[177: 281]. East Germany was a unique Cold War state because it was born of that conflict and died with it. On a day-to-day basis, it was repression in the guise of the SED, Stasi, People's Police and Berlin Wall that ensured stability. Secondly, most GDR citizens helped to sustain the regime by accepting it as an unalterable fact of life. Many participated in it; others remained apathetic [2: 167]. Both enabled the system to reproduce itself. According to Fulbrook, 'those born in the years 1925–32 seem to have been highly supportive of the GDR' [32: 185]. Thirdly, the very inefficiency of the totalitarian dictatorship helped to ensure its smoother functioning. As Port [174] and Madarász [130] have shown for the Ulbricht and Honecker periods, respectively, various compromises struck by the authorities prevented conflicts from turning into severe crises. Fourthly, antifascism helped to integrate the overwhelming majority of citizens who were not Communists. Fifthly, the SED's welfare policies provided some compensation for the negative aspects of the regime, particularly under Honecker. Although Port has shown that their inadequacy during the Ulbricht epoch was a key cause of popular dissatisfaction [174: 274], he neglects to mention that discontent would have been far greater without them. Between 1953 and the mid-1980s, welfare divided and then softened opposition to SED rule. Sixthly, Port has argued that social fragmentation, an unintended consequence of the party's policies, retarded the formation of popular opposition [174: 277–8, 283]. That said, his pioneering study is based solely on the southern industrial town of Saalfeld during the Ulbricht era. East German society became even more 'complex and differentiated' under Honecker [222: 387], but this did not save the system in 1989.

A Communist or a Socialist state?

A final question worth considering is whether or not East Germany can reasonably be described as 'Communist' or 'Socialist'. Some left-wing historians have attempted to disassociate these terms from the GDR, partly in order to salvage what remains of a discredited ideology. The Marxist scholar, Gareth Dale, for example, has described the Soviet bloc, of which the GDR was a member, as a 'state Capitalist formation' [34]. Yet the argument is reductionist because there was so much more to Marxist–Leninism than the state control and ownership of capital. What became known as 'communism' was not just an economic system; it was also a social and political one.

Those on the right often delight in attributing the failure of the 'Workers' and Peasants' Power' to 'socialism' or 'communism' (they use the words interchangeably). My own view is that the GDR cannot be characterized as 'Communist' in any meaningful sense. Even the SED never claimed to have built a Communist society while it was in power. Over the entire 40 years of its existence, the East German state hypertrophied. When it did finally 'wither away', as Marx prophesied, capitalism, not communism, ensued. Neither was Marx's dictum 'from each according to his abilities, to each according to his needs!'** fully realized in this society. In fact, a Marxist analysis, with its emphasis on the contradiction between base and superstructure, can help elucidate the GDR's systemic crisis.

As for 'socialism', that is another matter. What the SED built in East Germany was socialism without democracy, namely, distorted socialism. It nationalized the means of production, distribution, and exchange. It also created a more equal society by dramatically expanding welfare provision and levelling class differences. On the other hand, it destroyed many of the emancipatory features that were supposed to lie at the root of the Socialist idea. In 1893, Wilhelm Liebknecht, one of the leaders of the German labour movement, had declared the 'democratic state' to be 'the only possible basis upon which to organize a Socialist society' [220: 166]. Yet the so-called German Democratic Republic was really a totalitarian welfare dictatorship guaranteed by the Kremlin. It was hardly surprising, therefore, that the majority of its citizens eventually turned on their rulers or voted with their feet. In the end, what Communists described as 'People's Democracy' was overthrown by the very 'people' it claimed to represent.

Notes

* Leslie Poles Hartley, *The Go-Between* (London, 1953), p. 9.
♦ Gregory Andrusz, Michael Harloe and Ivan Szelenyi (eds), *Cities after Socialism: Urban and Regional Change and Conflict in Post-Socialist Societies* (Oxford, 1996), p. 218.
** Karl Marx, 'Critique of the Gotha Programme' in Karl Marx and Friedrich Engels, *Selected Works in One Volume* (London, Revised edn, 1991), p. 306.

Bibliography

[1]   Agde, Günter (ed.), *Kahlschlag: Das 11. Plenum des ZK der SED 1965. Studien und Dokumente* (Berlin, 1991).

[2]   Allinson, Mark, *Politics and Popular Opinion in East Germany, 1945–68* (Manchester, 2000).

[3]   Aly, Götz, *Hitler's Beneficiaries: How the Nazis Bought the German People* (London and NY, 2007).

[4]   Amos, Heike, *Die Westpolitik der SED, 1948/49–1961* (Berlin, 1999).

[5]   Andrew, Christopher and Vasili Mitrokhin, *The Mitrokhin Archive: The KGB in Europe and the West* (London, 2000).

[6]   Augustine, Dolores L., *Red Prometheus: Engineering and Dictatorship in East Germany, 1945–1990* (Cambridge, MA, 2007).

[7]   Badstübner, Rolf, Manfred Bensing, Jochen Černý, Gottfried Dittrich, Gerhard Keiderling, Willy Peter, Siegfried Prokop, Evemarie Badstübner-Peters, Harald Buttler, Siegfried Graffunder, Inge Melzer, *Geschichte der DDR* edited by Rolf Badstübner and Jochen Černý (East Berlin, 1984).

[8]   Balzer, Rolf, Günter Böhme, Ruth Eberhardt, Wolfgang Gitter, Wolfgang Heyl, Manfred Kirchhof, Günter Klein, Udo Krause, Dolf Künzel, Arnold Michl, Peter Niecke, Wolfgang Reischock, Klaus-Dieter Schönewerk, Otto Schoth, Hans-Gerd Schubert, Volkmar Stanke, Susanne Statkowa, *GDR – 100 Questions, 100 Answers*, edited by Lilli Piater and Irene Prutsch (Revised 2nd edn, East Berlin, 1975).

[9]   Baring, Arnulf, *Deutschland, was nun?* (Berlin, 1991).

[10] Baring, Arnulf, *Uprising in East Germany, June 17, 1953* (Ithaca, London, 1972).

[11] Barker, Peter, *Slavs in Germany: The Sorbian Minority and the German State since 1945* (NY, 2000).

[12] Bessel, Richard and Ralph Jessen (eds), *Die Grenzen der Diktatur: Staat und Gesellschaft in der DDR* (Göttingen, 1996).

[13] Betts, Paul, *Within Walls: Private Life in the German Democratic Republic* (Oxford, 2010).

[14] Blackbourn, David, *The Conquest of Nature: Water, Landscape, and the Making of Modern Germany* (London, 2006).

[15] Bohley, Bärbel, '"Under Open Skies": Reflections on German Unification' in *Bulletin of the German Historical Institute, Washington D. C.*, 42, Spring 2008, 27–37.

[16] Bollinger, Stefan and Fritz Vilmar (eds), *Die DDR war anders: Eine kritische Würdigung ihrer sozialkulturellen Einrichtungen* (Berlin, 2002).

[17] Boyce, Kate Elizabeth, 'Women's Discontent in the German Democratic Republic during the Honecker Era', University of Hull PhD Thesis, 2006.

[18] Braun, Jutta, 'The People's Sport? Popular Sport and Fans in the Later Years of the German Democratic Republic', *German History*, 27, 3, July 2009, 414–28.

[19] Bridge, Helen, *Women's Writing and Historiography in the GDR* (Oxford, 2002).

[20] Brinks, Jan Herman, 'Political Anti-fascism in the German Democratic Republic', *Journal of Contemporary History*, 32, 2, April, 1997, 207–17.

[21] Bruce, Gary, 'East Germany', *The Historical Journal*, 52, 3, 2009, 799–812.

[22] Bruce, Gary, *Resistance with the People: Repression and Resistance in Eastern Germany, 1945–1955* (Lanham, MD, 2003).

[23] Bruce, Gary, *The Firm: The Inside Story of the Stasi* (Oxford, 2010).

[24] Burgess, John, *The East German Church and the End of Communism* (NY, 1997).

[25] Burleigh, Michael, *Sacred Causes: Religion and Politics from the European Dictators to Al Qaeda* (London, 2007).

[26] Childs, David, *The Fall of the GDR: Germany's Road to Unity* (Harlow, 2001).

[27] Childs, David, *The GDR: Moscow's German Ally* (London, 1983).

[28] Childs, David and Richard Popplewell, *The Stasi: The East German Intelligence and Security Service* (Basingstoke, 1996).

[29] Connelly, John, *Captive University: The Sovietization of East German, Czech, and Polish Higher Education, 1945–1956* (Chapel Hill, 2000).

[30] Conway, John, 'The "Stasi" and the Churches: Between Coercion and Compromise in East German Protestantism, 1949–1989', *Journal of Church & State*, 36, 4, Autumn 1994.

[31] Cooke, Paul, *Representing East Germany since Unification: From Colonization to Nostalgia* (Oxford, 2005).

[32] Corner, Paul (ed.), *Popular Opinion in Totalitarian Regimes: Fascism, Nazism, Communism* (Oxford, 2009).

[33] Crampton, R. J., *Eastern Europe in the Twentieth Century – and After* (London, 2nd edn, 2003).

[34] Dale, Gareth, *Between State Capitalism and Globalization: The Collapse of the East German Economy* (Oxford, 2004).

[35] Dale, Gareth, *Popular Protest in East Germany, 1945–1989* (London, 2005).

[36] Dale, Gareth, *The East German Revolution of 1989* (Manchester, 2006).

[37] Dennis, Mike, *German Democratic Republic: Politics, Economics and Society* (London, 1988).

[38] Dennis, Mike, 'Surviving the Stasi: Jehovah's Witnesses in Communist East Germany, 1965 to 1989', *Religion, State and Society*, 34, 2, June 2006, 145–68.

[39]   Dennis, Mike, *The Rise and Fall of the German Democratic Republic,*
        1945–1990 (Harlow, 2000).

[40]   Dennis, Mike, *The Stasi: Myth and Reality* (Harlow, 2003).

[41]   *Die besten Witze aus der DDR* (Vienna, 2003).

[42]   Diedrich, Torsten, *Der 17. Juni 1953 in der DDR: Bewaffnete Gewalt*
        gegen das Volk (Berlin, 1991).

[43]   Diedrich, Torsten, *Waffen gegen das Volk: Der 17 Juni 1953 in der DDR*
        (Munich, 2003).

[44]   Djilas, Milovan, *Conversations with Stalin* (Harmondsworth, 1967).

[45]   Dockrill, Michael L. and Michael F. Hopkins, *The Cold War,*
        1945–1991 (Basingstoke, 2nd edn, 2006).

[46]   Eisenberg, Carolyn, *Drawing the Line: The American Decision to Divide*
        Germany, 1944–1949 (Cambridge, 1996).

[47]   Epstein, Catherine, *The Last Revolutionaries: German Communists and*
        their Century (Cambridge, MA, 2003).

[48]   Epstein, Catherine, 'The Stasi: New Research on the East German
        Ministry of State Security', *Kritika: Explorations in Russian and*
        Eurasian History, 5.2, Spring 2004, 321–48.

[49]   Fenemore, Mark, *Sex, Thugs and Rock 'n' Roll: Teenage Rebels in Cold-*
        War East Germany (NY and Oxford, 2009).

[50]   Frank, Mario, *Walter Ulbricht: Eine deutsche Biografie* (Berlin, 2001).

[51]   Fricke, Karl Wilhelm, *Die DDR-Staatssicherheit: Entwicklung, Struktu-*
        ren, Aktionsfelder (Cologne, 1984).

[52]   Fricke, Karl Wilhelm, *Opposition und Widerstand in der DDR: Ein poli-*
        tischer Report (Cologne, 1984).

[53]   Fricke, Karl Wilhelm, *Selbstbehauptung und Widerstand in der Sowjeti-*
        schen Besatzungszone Deutschlands (Bonn, 1964).

[54]   Friedrich, Carl and Zbigniew Brzezinski, *Totalitarian Dictatorship*
        and Autocracy (Cambridge, MA, 1956).

[55]   Friedrich, Carl, Michael Curtis and Benjamin Barber (eds), *Totali-*
        tarianism in Perspective: Three Views (NY, 1969).

[56]   Friedrich, Wolfgang-Uwe (ed.), *Die totalitäre Herrschaft der SED: Wirk-*
        lichkeit und Nachwirkungen (Munich, 1998).

[57]   Führer, Christian, *Und wir sind dabei gewesen: Die Revolution, die aus*
        der Kirche kam (Berlin, 2009).

[58]   Fulbrook, Mary, 'A German Dictatorship: Power Structures and Polit-
        ical Culture', *German Life and Letters*, 45:4, October 1992, 376–92.

[59]   Fulbrook, Mary, *Anatomy of a Dictatorship: Inside the GDR, 1949–1989*
        (Oxford, 1995).

[60]   Fulbrook, Mary, *German National Identity after the Holocaust*
        (Cambridge, 1999).

[61]   Fulbrook, Mary (ed.), *Power and Society in the GDR, 1961–1979:*
        A 'Normalization of Rule'? (NY and Oxford, 2009).

[62]   Fulbrook, Mary, 'Putting the People Back In: The Contentious State
        of GDR History', *German History*, 24, 4, November 2006, 608–20.

[63]   Fulbrook, Mary, 'The Limits of Totalitarianism: God, State and
        Society in the GDR', *Transactions of the Royal Historical Society*, VII,
        1997, 25–52.

[64] Fulbrook, Mary, *The People's State: East German Society from Hitler to Honecker* (London, 2005).

[65] Funder, Anna, *Stasiland* (London, 2003).

[66] Gaddis, John Lewis, *The Cold War* (London, 2005).

[67] Garthoff, Raymond L., *Détente and Confrontation: American-Soviet Relations from Nixon to Reagan* (Revised edn, Washington, 1994).

[68] Garton Ash, Timothy, *Facts are Subversive: Political Writing from a Decade without a Name* (London, 2009).

[69] Garton Ash, Timothy, *In Europe's Name: Germany and the Divided Continent* (London, 1993).

[70] Garton Ash, Timothy, *The File: A Personal History* (London, 1997).

[71] Garton Ash, Timothy, *The Magic Lantern: The Revolution of '89 witnessed in Warsaw, Budapest, Berlin, and Prague* (NY, 1999).

[72] Gassert, Philipp and Martin Klimke (ed.), '1968: Memories and Legacies of a Global Revolt', *Bulletin of the German Historical Institute*, Washington D. C., 6, 2009.

[73] Gaus, Günter, *Wo Deutschland liegt* (Hamburg, 1983).

[74] Geppert, Dominik, *Störmanöver: Das „Manifest der Opposition" und die Schließung des Ost-Berliner „Spiegel"-Büros im Januar 1978* (Berlin, 1996).

[75] Glaeßner, Gert-Joachim and Ian Wallace (eds), *The German Revolution of 1989: Causes and Consequences* (Oxford and Providence, 1992).

[76] Glees, Anthony, *The Stasi Files: East Germany's Secret Operations against Britain* (London, 2003).

[77a] Gniffke, Erich W., *Jahre mit Ulbricht* (Cologne, 1990).

[77b] Gorbachev, Mikhail, *Wie es war: Die deutsche Wiedervereinigung* (Munich, 2000).

[78] Granick, David, *Enterprise Guidance in Eastern Europe: A Comparison of Four Socialist Economies* (Princeton, NJ, 1975).

[79] Granville, Johanna, 'Ulbricht in October 1956: Survival of the Spitzbart during De-Stalinization', *Journal of Contemporary History*, 41, 3, July, 2006, 477–502.

[80] Grashoff, Udo, *'In einem Anfall von Depression ...' Selbsttötungen in der DDR* (Berlin, 2006).

[81] Gregor, Neil (ed.), *Nazism* (Oxford, 2000).

[82] Grieder, Peter, 'In Defence of Totalitarianism Theory as a Tool of Historical Scholarship', *Totalitarian Movements and Political Religions*, 8:3, 2007, 563–89.

[83a] Grieder, Peter, 'Perspectives on *Resistance with the People*', *Journal of Cold War Studies*, 9, 3, 2007, 149–54.

[83b] Grieder, Peter, 'Review of *Driving the Soviets up the Wall: Soviet-East German Relations, 1953–1961* by Hope M. Harrison', *Central European History*, 38, 4, 2005, 710–12.

[84] Grieder, Peter, *The East German Leadership, 1946–1973: Conflict and Crisis* (Manchester, 1999).

[85] Grix, Jonathan, *The Role of the Masses in the Collapse of the GDR* (Basingstoke, 2000).

[86] Habermas, Jürgen, *Die nachholende Revolution* (Frankfurt a.M., 1990).

[87]   Hagen, Manfred, *DDR – Juni '53: Die erste Volkserhebung im Stalinismus* (Stuttgart, 1992).

[88]   Harrison, Hope M., *Driving the Soviets up the Wall: Soviet-East German Relations, 1953–1961* (Princeton, NJ, 2003).

[89]   Harsch, Donna, 'Society, the State, and Abortion in East Germany, 1950–1972', *The American Historical Review*, 102, 1, February, 1997, 53–84.

[90]   Havel, Václav, *Václav Havel or Living in Truth: Twenty-two Essays Published on the Occasion of the Award of the Erasmus Prize to Václav Havel*, edited by Jan Vladislav (London, 1989).

[91]   Hegedüs, András and Manfred Wilke (eds), *Satelliten nach Stalins Tod* (Berlin, 2000).

[92]   Herf, Jeffrey, *Divided Memory: The Nazi Past in the Two Germanys* (Cambridge, MA, 1997).

[93]   Herrnstadt, Rudolf, *Das Herrnstadt-Dokument: Das Politburo der SED und die Geschichte des 17 Juni 1953*, edited by Nadja Stulz-Herrnstadt (Reinbek bei Hamburg, 1991).

[94]   Hertle, Hans-Hermann and Stefan Wolle, *Damals in der DDR: Der Alltag im Arbeiter- und Bauernstaat* (Munich, 2004).

[95]   Hobsbawm, Eric, *Age of Extremes: The Short Twentieth Century, 1914–1991* (London, 1995).

[96]   Hobsbawm, Eric, *Interesting Times: A Twentieth-Century Life* (London, 2002).

[97]   Hurwitz, Harold, with the assistance of Ursula Böhme and Andreas Malycha, *Die Stalinisierung der SED: Zum Verlust von Freiräumen und sozialdemokratischer Identität in den Vorständen 1946–1949* (Opladen, 1997).

[98]   Jarausch, Konrad H., (ed.), *Dictatorship as Experience: Towards a Socio-Cultural History of the GDR* (Oxford, 1999).

[99]   Jarausch, Konrad H., *The Rush to German Unity* (NY, 1994).

[100]   Jesse, Eckhard, 'War die DDR totalitär?', *Aus Politik und Zeitgeschichte*, B40/94, 7 October 1994, 12–23.

[101]   Jessen, Ralph, *Akademische Elite und kommunistische Diktatur: Die ostdeutsche Hochschullehrerschaft in der Ulbricht Ära* (Göttingen, 1999).

[102]   Johnson, Molly Wilkinson, *Training Socialist Citizens: Sports and the State in East Germany* (Leiden, 2008).

[103]   Judt, Tony, *Postwar: A History of Europe since 1945* (London, 2005).

[104]   Kaelbe, Hartmut, Jürgen Kocka and Hartmut Zwahr (eds), *Sozialgeschichte der DDR* (Stuttgart, 1994).

[105]   Kaiser, Monika, *1972 – Knockout für den Mittelstand: Zum Wirken von SED, CDU, LDPD und NDPD für die Verstaatlichung der Klein- und Mittelbetriebe* (Berlin, 1990).

[106]   Kaiser, Monika, *Machtwechsel von Ulbricht zu Honecker: Funktionsmechanismen der SED-Diktatur in Konfliktsituationen, 1962 bis 1972* (Berlin, 1997).

[107] Kettenacker, Lothar, *Germany 1989: In the Aftermath of the Cold War* (Harlow, 2009).

[108] Klein, Thomas, Wilfriede Otto and Peter Grieder, *Visionen, Repression und Opposition in der SED (1949–1989)* (Revised 2nd edn, Frankfurt/Oder, 1997).

[109] Klemperer, Victor, *The Lesser Evil: The Diaries of Victor Klemperer, 1945–59* (London, 2003).

[110] Kneipp, Danuta, *Im Abseits: Berufliche Diskriminierung und politische Dissidenz in der Honecker-DDR* (Cologne, 2009).

[111] Kocka, Jürgen, 'Ein deutscher Sonderweg: Überlegungen zur Sozialgeschichte der DDR', *Aus Politik und Zeitgeschichte*, B40/94, 7 October 1994, 34–45.

[112] Koehler, John O., *Stasi: The Untold Story of the East German Secret Police* (Boulder, CO, 1999).

[113] Koop, Volker, *Der 17 Juni 1953: Legende und Wirklichkeit* (Berlin, 2003).

[114] Kopstein, Jeffrey, *The Politics of Economic Decline in East Germany, 1945–1989* (Chapel Hill, 1997).

[115] Kowalczuk, Ilko-Sascha, Armin Mitter and Stefan Wolle, *Der Tag X – 17 Juni 1953: Die 'Innere' Staatsgründung der DDR als Ergebnis der Krise 1952/54* (Berlin, 1995).

[116] Kowalczuk, Ilko-Sascha, *17.6.1953 – Volksaufstand in der DDR: Ursachen, Abläufe, Folgen* (Bremen, 2003).

[117] Kowalczuk, Ilko-Sascha, *Endspiel: Die Revolution von 1989 in der DDR* (Munich, 2009).

[118] Landsman, Mark, *Dictatorship and Demand: The Politics of Consumerism in East Germany* (Cambridge, MA, 2005).

[119] Large, David Clay, *Berlin* (NY, 2000).

[120] Leeder, Karen, *Breaking Boundaries: A New Generation of Poets in the GDR* (Oxford, 1996).

[121] Lemke, Michael, *Einheit oder Sozialismus? Die Deutschlandpolitik der SED 1949–1961* (Cologne, 2001).

[122] Leonhard, Wolfgang, *Das kurze Leben der DDR: Berichte und Kommentare aus vier Jahrzehnten* (Stuttgart, 1990).

[123] Leonhard, Wolfgang, *Die Revolution entlässt ihre Kinder* (Cologne, 1992 edn).

[124] Lewkowicz, Nicolas, *The German Question and the International Order, 1943–48* (Basingstoke, 2010).

[125] Lindenberger, Thomas, 'Herrschaft und Eigen-Sinn in der Diktatur: Das Alltagsleben der DDR und sein Platz in der Erinnerungskultur des vereinten Deutschlands', *Aus Politik und Zeitgeschichte*, B40/2000, 29 September 2000, 5–12.

[126] Linz, Juan, *Totalitarian and Authoritarian Regimes* (Boulder, CO, 2000).

[127] Loth, Wilfried, *Die Sowjetunion und die deutsche Frage: Studien zur sowjetischen Deutschlandpolitik* (Göttingen, 2007).

[128] Loth, Wilfried, *Stalins ungeliebtes Kind: Warum Moskau die DDR nicht wollte* (Berlin, 1994).

[129]   Ludz, Peter, *The Changing Party Elite in East Germany* (Cambridge, MA, 1972).

[130]   Madarász, Jeannette Z., *Conflict and Compromise in East Germany, 1971–1989: A Precarious Stability* (Basingstoke, 2003).

[131]   Madarász, Jeannette Z., *Working in East Germany: Normality in a Socialist Dictatorship, 1961–79* (Basingstoke, 2006).

[132]   Maddrell, Paul, 'The Western Secret Services, the East German Ministry of State Security and the Building of the Berlin Wall', *Intelligence and National Security*, 21, 5, October 2006, 829–47.

[133]   Maier, Charles S., *Dissolution: The Crisis of Communism and the End of East Germany* (Princeton, NJ, 1999).

[134]   Major, Patrick and Jonathan Osmond (eds), *The Workers' and Peasants' State: Communism and Society in East Germany under Ulbricht, 1945–71* (Manchester, 2002).

[135]   Major, Patrick, *Behind the Berlin Wall: East Germany and the Frontiers of Power* (Oxford, 2010).

[136]   Malycha, Andreas, *Die SED: Geschichte ihrer Stalinisierung, 1946–1953* (Paderborn, 2000).

[137]   Malycha, Andreas, *Partei von Stalins Gnaden? Die Entwicklung der SED zur Partei neuen Typus in den Jahren 1946 bis 1950* (Berlin, 1996).

[138]   Mampel, Siegfried, *Totalitäres Hersschaftssystem* (Berlin, 2001).

[139]   Markovits, Inga, *Justice in Lüritz: Experiencing Socialist Law in East Germany* (NJ, 2010).

[140]   Marshall, Barbara, *Willy Brandt: A Political Biography* (Basingstoke and Oxford, 1997).

[141]   Maurin, Jost, 'Die DDR als Asylland: Flüchtlinge aus Chile, 1973–1989', *Zeitschrift für Geschichtswissenschaft*, 51.9, 2003, 814–31.

[142]   McAdams, A. James, *East Germany and Détente: Building Authority after the Wall* (Cambridge, 1985).

[143]   McAdams, A. James, *Germany Divided: From the Wall to Reunification* (Princeton, NJ, 1994).

[144]   McCauley, Martin, *The German Democratic Republic since 1945* (London, 1983).

[145]   McDermott, Kevin and Matthew Stibbe (eds), *Revolution and Resistance in Eastern Europe: Challenges to Communist Rule* (Oxford and NY, 2006).

[146]   McDermott, Kevin and Matthew Stibbe (eds), *Stalinist Terror in Eastern Europe: Elite Purges and Mass Repression* (Manchester, 2010).

[147]   McDougall, Alan, *Youth Politics in East Germany: The Free German Youth Movement, 1946–1968* (Oxford, 2004).

[148]   McElvoy, Anne, *The Saddled Cow: East Germany's Life and Legacy* (London, 1993).

[149]   McLellan, Josie, *Anti-fascism and Memory in East Germany: Remembering the International Brigades, 1945–1989* (Oxford, 2004).

[150]   McLellan, Josie, 'State Socialist Bodies: East German Nudism from Ban to Boom', *Journal of Modern History*, 79, March 2007, 48–79.

[151]   Meuschel, Sigrid, *Legitimation und Parteiherrschaft in der DDR: Zum Paradox von Stabilität und Revolution in der DDR, 1945–1989* (Frankfurt a.M., 1992).

[152]   Mitter, Armin and Stefan Wolle, *Untergang auf Raten: Unbekannte Kapitel der DDR-Geschichte* (Munich, 1993).

[153]   Molloy, Peter, *The Lost World of Communism: An Oral History of Daily Life Behind the Iron Curtain* (London, 2009).

[154]   Naimark, Norman M., *The Russians in Germany: A History of the Soviet Zone of Occupation, 1945–1949* (Cambridge, MA, 1995).

[155]   Nakath, Monika, 'SED und Perestroika: Reflexion osteuropäischer Reformversuche in den 80er Jahren', *Hefte zur DDR-Geschichte* (Berlin, 1993).

[156]   Naumann, Gerhard and Eckhard Trümpler, *Der Flop mit der DDR-Nation 1971* (Berlin, 1991).

[157]   Naumann, Gerhard and Eckhard Trümpler, *Von Ulbricht zu Honecker: 1970 – ein Krisenjahr der DDR* (Berlin, 1990).

[158]   Nelson, Arvid, *Cold War Ecology: Forests, Farms, & People in the East German Landscape, 1945–1989* (New Haven, 2005).

[159]   Nettl, J. P., *The Eastern Zone and Soviet Policy in Germany, 1945–50* (London, 1951).

[160]   Neubert, E., 'Protestantische Kultur und DDR-Revolution', *Aus Politik und Zeitgeschichte*, 19, 3 May 1991, 21–9.

[161a] Neumann, Thomas, *Die Maßnahme: Eine Herrschaftsgeschichte der SED* (Reinbek bei Hamburg, 1991).

[161b] Nicholls, A. J., 'Historians and Totalitarianism: The Impact of German Unification', *Journal of Contemporary History*, 36, 4, October 2001, 653–61.

[162]   Niven, Bill (ed.), *Germans as Victims: Remembering the Past in Contemporary Germany* (Basingstoke, 2006).

[163]   Nothnagle, Alan L., *Building the East German Myth: Historical Mythology and Youth Propaganda in the German Democratic Republic, 1945–1989* (Ann Arbor, 1999).

[164]   O'Doherty, Paul, 'The GDR in the Context of Stalinist Show Trials and Anti-Semitism in Eastern Europe, 1948–54', *German History*, 10, 3, 1992, 302–17.

[165]   Orlow, Dietrich, 'The GDR's Failed Search for a National Identity, 1945–1989', *German Studies Review*, 29, 3, October, 2006, 537–58.

[166]   Ostermann, Christian, *Uprising in East Germany 1953: The Cold War, the German Question, and the First Major Upheaval behind the Iron Curtain* (Budapest, 2001).

[167]   Overy, Richard, *The Dictators: Hitler's Germany and Stalin's Russia* (London, 2004).

[168]   Palmowski, Jan, *Inventing a Socialist Nation: Heimat and the Politics of Everyday Life in the GDR, 1945–1990* (Cambridge, 2009).

[169]   Parkes, Stuart, *Understanding Contemporary Germany* (London, 1997).

[170]   Pence, Katherine and Paul Betts (eds), *Socialist Modern: East German Everyday Culture and Politics* (Ann Arbor, 2008).

[171]   Peterson, Edward, *The Secret Police and the Revolution: The Fall of the German Democratic Republic* (Westport, CT, 2001).

[172]   Pfeiler, Wolfgang, 'Das Deutschlandbild und die Deutschland-politik Josef Stalins', *Deutschland Archiv*, November 1979, 1258–82.

[173]   Pommerin, Reiner, 'Die Zwangsvereinigung von KPD und SPD zur SED: Eine britische Analyse vom April 1946', *Vierteljahrshefte für Zeitgeschichte*, 36: 2, April 1988, 319–38.

[174]   Port, Andrew, *Conflict and Stability in the German Democratic Republic* (Cambridge, 2009).

[175]   Priestland, David, *The Red Flag: Communism and the Making of the Modern World* (London, 2010).

[176]   Pritchard, Gareth, *The Making of the GDR, 1945–53: From Antifascism to Stalinism* (Manchester, 2000).

[177]   Przybylski, Peter, *Tatort Politbüro: Die Akte Honecker* (Berlin, 1991).

[178]   Przybylski, Peter, *Tatort Politbüro. Band 2: Honecker, Mittag und Schalck-Golodkowski* (Berlin, 1992).

[179]   Pulzer, Peter, *German Politics, 1945–1995* (Oxford, 1995).

[180]   Raack, R. C., *Stalin's Drive to the West, 1938–1945: The Origins of the Cold War* (Stanford, CA, 1995).

[181]   Rein, Gerhard, *Die protestantische Revolution, 1987–1990: Ein deutsches Lesebuch* (Berlin, 1997).

[182]   Richie, Alexandra, *Faust's Metropolis: A History of Berlin* (London, 1999).

[183]   Richthofen, Esther von, *Bringing Culture to the Masses: Control, Compromise and Participation in the GDR* (New York and Oxford, 2009).

[184]   Roberts, G., 'A Chance for Peace? The Soviet Campaign to End the Cold War, 1953–1955', *Cold War International History Project Bulletin*, Working Paper 57, December 2008.

[185]   Roesler, Jörg, 'Das Neue Ökonomische System – Dekorations-oder Paradigmenwechsel?', *Hefte zur DDR-Geschichte* (Berlin, 1993).

[186]   Roesler, Jörg, *Zwischen Plan und Markt: Die Wirtschaftsreform 1963–1970 in der DDR* (Berlin, 1991).

[187]   Ross, Corey, 'Before the Wall: East Germans, Communist Authority, and the Mass Exodus to the West', *The Historical Journal*, 45, 2, June, 2002, 459–80.

[188]   Ross, Corey, *Constructing Socialism at the Grass-Roots: The Transformation of East Germany, 1945–65* (Basingstoke, 2000).

[189]   Ross, Corey, 'East Germans and the Berlin Wall: Popular Opinion and Social Change before and after the Border Closure of August 1961', *Journal of Contemporary History*, 39, 1, 2004, 25–43.

[190]   Ross, Corey, *The East German Dictatorship: Problems and Perspectives in the Interpretation of the GDR* (London, 2002).

[191]   Rubin, Eli, *Synthetic Socialism: Plastics and Dictatorship in the German Democratic Republic* (Chapel Hill, 2008).

[192]   Salmon, Patrick, Keith Hamilton and Stephen Robert Twigge (eds), *German Unification 1989–90: Documents on British Policy Overseas*, Series III, Volume VII (London, 2010).

[193]   Sarotte, M. E., *Dealing with the Devil: East Germany, Détente, and Ostpolitik, 1969–1973* (Chapel Hill, 2001).

[194]   Saunders, Anna, *Honecker's Children: Youth and Patriotism in East(ern) Germany, 1979–2002* (Manchester, 2007).

[195]   Schmeidel, John C., *Stasi: Shield and Sword of the Party* (London and NY, 2008).

[196]   Schroeder, Klaus, *Der SED-Staat: Partei, Staat und Gesellschaft, 1949–1990* (Munich, 1998).

[197]   Selbourne, David, *Death of the Dark Hero: Eastern Europe, 1987–1990* (London, 2009).

[198]   Smyser, W. R., *From Yalta to Berlin: The Cold War Struggle over Germany* (Basingstoke, 1999).

[199]   Sodaro, Michael, *Moscow, Germany and the West from Khrushchev to Gorbachev* (Ithaca, 1991).

[200]   Sperber, Jonathan, '17 June 1953: Revisiting a Revolution', *German History*, 22, 4, November 2004, 619–43.

[201]   Spilker, Dirk, *The East German Leadership and the Division of Germany: Patriotism and Propaganda 1945–1953* (Oxford, 2006).

[202]   Staadt, Jochen, 'Walter Ulbrichts letzter Machtkampf', *Deutschland Archiv*, 29, 1996, 686–700.

[203]   Staritz, Dietrich, 'Ein "besonderer deutscher Weg" zum Sozialismus?', *Aus Politik und Zeitgeschichte*, B 51–2, 1982, 15–31.

[204]   Staritz, Dietrich, *Geschichte der DDR, 1949–1985* (Frankfurt a.M., 1985).

[205]   Staritz, Dietrich, 'The SED, Stalin, and the German Question: Interests and Decision-Making in the Light of New Sources', *German History*, 10, 3, 1992, 274–89.

[206]   Steege, Paul, *Black Market, Cold War: Everyday Life in Berlin, 1946–1949* (Cambridge, 2007).

[207]   Steele, Jonathan, *Socialism with a German Face: The State that Came in From the Cold* (London, 1977).

[208]   Steiner, André, *The Plans That Failed: An Economic History of the GDR* (NY, 2010).

[209]   Stelkens, Jochen, 'Machtwechsel in Ost-Berlin: Der Sturz Walter Ulbrichts 1971', *Vierteljahrshefte für Zeitgeschichte*, 45, 1997, 503–33.

[210]   Sywottek, Arnold, '"Stalinismus" und "Totalitarismus" in der DDR-Geschichte', *Deutsche Studien*, 30/117–118, 1993, 25–38.

[211]   Taylor, Frederick, *The Berlin Wall, 13 August 1961 – 9 November 1989* (London, 2006).

[212]   Thomaneck, J. K. A. and Bill Niven, *Dividing and Uniting Germany* (London, 2001).

[213]   Thomas, Merrilyn, *Communing with the Enemy: Covert Operations, Christianity and Cold War Politics in Britain and the GDR* (Oxford, 2005).

[214]   Timm, Angelika, *Jewish Claims against East Germany: Moral Obligations and Pragmatic Policy* (Budapest, 1998).

[215]   Turner, Henry Ashby, *Germany from Partition to Reunification* (New Haven, CT, 1992).

[216]   'Umfrage: Die DDR hat noch immer jede Menge Anhänger', *Die Welt*, 27 June 2009, *Welt Online*: http://www.welt.de/die-welt/article4010147/Umfrage-Die-DDR-hat-noch-immer-jede-Menge-Anhaenger.html. Last accessed 17 February 2012.

[217]   Vinen, Richard, *A History in Fragments: Europe in the Twentieth Century* (London, 2000).

[218]   Vollnhals, Clemens and Jürgen Weber (eds), *Der Schein der Normalität: Alltag und Herrschaft in der SED-Diktatur* (Munich, 2002).

[219]   Weber, Hermann, *Aufbau und Fall einer Diktatur: Kritische Beiträge zur Geschichte der DDR* (Cologne, 1991).

[220]   Weber, Hermann, *DDR: Grundriß der Geschichte, 1945–1990* (Hannover, 1991).

[221]   Weber, Hermann, *Geschichte der DDR* (Munich, 1985).

[222]   Weitz, Eric D., *Creating German Communism, 1890–1990: From Popular Protests to Socialist State* (Princeton, NJ, 1997).

[223]   Wettig, Gerhard, *Bereitschaft zu Einheit in Freiheit? Die sowjetische Deutschland-Politik 1945–1955* (Munich, 1999).

[224]   Wilke, Manfred and Michael Kubina, '"Die Lage in Polen ist schlimmer als 1968 in der ČSSR ...": Die Forderung des SED-Politbüros nach einer Intervention in Polen im Herbst 1980', *Deutschland Archiv*, 3, 1993, 335–40.

[225]   Witkowski, Gregory, 'Peasants Revolt? Re-evaluating the 17 June Uprising in East Germany', *German History*, 24, 2, May 2006, 243–66.

[226]   Wolf, Markus with Anne McElvoy, *Man without a Face: The Autobiography of Communism's Greatest Spymaster* (NY, 1997).

[227]   Wolle, Stefan, *Der Traum von der Revolte: Die DDR 1968* (Berlin, 2008).

[228]   Wolle, Stefan, *Die heile Welt der Diktatur: Alltag und Herrschaft in der DDR, 1971–1989* (Revised 3rd edn, Berlin, 2009).

[229]   Woods, Roger, *Opposition in the GDR under Honecker, 1971–85: An Introduction and Documentation* (Basingstoke, 1986).

[230]   Zatlin, Jonathan R., *The Currency of Socialism: Money and Political Culture in East Germany* (Cambridge, 2009).

Index

DATE DUE
